POWER *of the* SUPER MIND

Since its publication in 1937, Napoleon Hill's seminal *Think and Grow Rich* has inspired generations of readers to develop their skills and become masters at anything to do. Inspired by Andrew Carnegie himself, Hill's easy-to-follow guidebook to success is based on thirteen simple 'steps': 1. Desire 2. Faith 3. Autosuggestion 4. Specialized Knowledge 5. Imagination 6. Organized Planning 7. Decision 8. Persistence 9. Power of the Master Mind 10. The Mystery of Sex Transmutation 11. The Subconscious Mind 12. The Brain 13. The Sixth Sense. Through a mixture of sound advice, income management methods, and personal anecdotes, Hill delivers the ultimate motivational message in *Think and Grow Rich*—and probably the only one you'll ever need. Discover for yourself what makes this guidebook to better living one of the bestselling books of all time!

'A man's wealth is not in the coins he carries in his purse; it is the income he builds, the golden stream that continually flows into his purse and keeps it always bulging.' This 1926 classic serves as a talisman through its renowned collection of Babylonian parables for those seeking financial wisdom and stability in life. Its powerhouse of time-tested principles on how to gain and retain wealth has been inspiring finances, it also discusses the 'five laws of gold' and provides us with insights on not only how to be in clover but also keep good luck at one's side. Even after almost 100 years of *The Richest Man in Babylon*, it continues to remain a classic bestseller.

In the international bestseller book, *The Science of Getting Rich*, Wallace D. Wattles provides us with a unique practical guide to achieving economic and emotional security in our lives. He provides us with practical principles which are embedded in science and philosophy, and a plan of action that will help create a harmonious environment for ourselves, complete with wealth, wisdom and happiness.

POWER *of the* SUPER MIND

The Ultimate Guide to Getting Richer

NAPOLEON HILL
GEORGE S. CLASON
WALLACE D. WATTLES

RUPA

Published by
Rupa Publications India Pvt. Ltd 2023
7/16, Ansari Road, Daryaganj
New Delhi 110002

Sales Centres:
Bengaluru Chennai Hyderabad
Jaipur Kathmandu Kolkata
Mumbai Prayagraj

P-ISBN: 978-93-5702-674-1
E-ISBN: 978-93-5702-862-2

First impression 2023

10 9 8 7 6 5 4 3 2 1

Printed in India

CONTENTS

THINK AND GROW RICH

Since its publication in 1937, Napoleon Hill's seminal Think and Grow Rich has inspired generations of readers to develop their skills and become masters at anything to do. Inspired by Andrew Carnegie himself, Hill's easy-to-follow guidebook to success is based on thirteen simple 'steps': 1. Desire 2. Faith 3. Autosuggestion 4. Specialized Knowledge 5. Imagination 6. Organized Planning 7. Decision 8. Persistence 9. Power of the Master Mind 10. The Mystery of Sex Transmutation 11. The Subconscious Mind 12. The Brain 13. The Sixth Sense. Through a mixture of sound advice, income management methods, and personal anecdotes, Hill delivers the ultimate motivational message in *Think and Grow Rich*—and probably the only one you'll ever need. Discover for yourself what makes this guidebook to better living one of the bestselling books of all time!

1

DESIRE
The Starting Point of All Achievement

THE FIRST STEP TOWARD RICHES

When Edwin C. Barnes climbed down from the freight train in Orange, N.J., more than thirty years ago, he may have resembled a tramp, but his *thoughts* were those of a king!

As he made his way from the railroad tracks to Thomas A. Edison's office, his mind was at work. He saw himself *standing in Edison's presence*. He heard himself asking Mr Edison for an opportunity to carry out the one CONSUMING OBSESSION OF HIS LIFE, a BURNING DESIRE to become the business associate of the great inventor.

Barnes' desire was not a *hope*! It was not a *wish*! It was a keen, pulsating DESIRE, which transcended everything else. It was DEFINITE.

The desire was not new when he approached Edison. It had been Barnes' *dominating desire* for a long time. In the beginning, when the desire first appeared in his mind, it may have been, probably was, only a wish, but it was no mere wish when he appeared before Edison with it.

A few years later, Edwin C. Barnes again stood before Edison, in the same office where he first met the inventor. This time his DESIRE had been translated into reality. *He was in business with Edison*. The dominating DREAM OF HIS LIFE had become a reality. Today, people who know Barnes envy him, because of the 'break' life yielded him. They see him in the days of his triumph, without taking the trouble to investigate the *cause* of his success.

Barnes succeeded because he chose a definite goal, placed all his energy, all his will power, all his effort, everything back of that goal. He did not become the partner of Edison the day he arrived. He was content to start in the most menial work, as long as it provided an opportunity to take even one step toward his cherished goal.

Five years passed before the chance he had been seeking made its appearance. During all those years not one ray of hope, not one promise of attainment of his DESIRE had been held out to him. To everyone, except himself, he appeared only another cog in the Edison business wheel, but in his own mind, HE WAS THE PARTNER OF EDISON EVERY MINUTE OF THE TIME, from the very day that he first went to work there.

It is a remarkable illustration of the power of a DEFINITE DESIRE. Barnes won his goal, because he wanted to be a business associate of Mr Edison, more than he wanted anything else. He created a plan by which to attain that purpose.

But he BURNED ALL BRIDGES BEHIND HIM.

He stood by his DESIRE until it became the dominating

obsession of his life—and—finally, a fact.

When he went to Orange, he did not say to himself, 'I will try to induce

Edison to give me a job of some soft.' He said, 'I will see Edison, and put him on notice that I have come to go into business with him.

He did not say, 'I will work there for a few months, and if I get no encouragement, I will quit and get a job somewhere else.' He did say, 'I will start anywhere. I will do anything Edison tells me to do, but *before I am through*, I will be his associate.'

He did not say, 'I will keep my eyes open for another opportunity, in case I fail to get what I want in the Edison organization.' He said, 'There is but ONE thing in this world that I am determined to have, and that is a business association with Thomas A. Edison. I will burn all bridges behind me, and stake my ENTIRE FUTURE on my ability to get what I want.'

He left himself no possible way of retreat. He had to win or perish!

That is all there is to the Barnes story of success! A long while ago, a great warrior faced a situation which made it necessary for him to make a decision which insured his success on the battlefield. He was about to send his armies against a powerful foe, whose men outnumbered his own. He loaded his soldiers into boats, sailed to the enemy's country, unloaded soldiers and equipment, then gave the order to burn the ships that had carried them. Addressing his men before the first battle, he said, 'You see the boats going up in smoke. That means that we cannot leave these shores alive unless we win! We now have no choice—*we win, or we perish!* They won.

Every person who wins in any undertaking must be willing

to burn his ships and cut all sources of retreat. Only by so doing can one be sure of maintaining that state of mind known as a BURNING DESIRE TO WIN, essential to success.

The morning after the great Chicago fire, a group of merchants stood on State Street, looking at the smoking remains of what had been their stores. They went into a conference to decide if they would try to rebuild, or leave Chicago and start over in a more promising section of the country. They reached a decision—all except one—to leave Chicago.

The merchant who decided to stay and rebuild pointed a finger at the remains of his store, and said, 'Gentlemen, on that very spot I will build the world's greatest store, no matter how many times it may burn down.'

That was more than fifty years ago. The store was built. It stands there today, a towering monument to the power of that state of mind known as a BURNING DESIRE. The easy thing for Marshal Field to have done, would have been exactly what his fellow merchants did. When the going was hard, and the future looked dismal, they pulled up and went where the going seemed easier.

Mark well this difference between Marshal Field and the other merchants, because it is the same difference which distinguishes Edwin C. Barnes from thousands of other young men who have worked in the Edison organization. It is the same difference which distinguishes practically all who succeed from those who fail.

Every human being who reaches the age of understanding of the purpose of money, wishes for it. *Wishing* will not bring riches. But *desiring* riches with a state of mind that becomes an obsession, then planning definite ways and means to acquire riches, and backing those plans with persistence which *does not recognize failure*, will bring riches.

The method by which DESIRE for riches can be transmuted into its financial equivalent, consists of six definite, practical steps, viz:

First: Fix in your mind the *exact* amount of money you desire. It is not sufficient merely to say 'I want plenty of money.' Be definite as to the amount. (There is a psychological reason for definiteness which will be described in a subsequent chapter).

Second: Determine exactly what you intend to give in return for the money you desire. (There is no such reality as 'something for nothing'.)

Third: Establish a definite date when you intend to *possess* the money you desire.

Fourth: Create a definite plan for carrying out your desire, and begin *at once*, whether you are ready or not, to put this plan into *action*.

Fifth: Write out a clear, concise statement of the amount of money you intend to acquire, name the time limit for its acquisition, state what you intend to give in return for the money, and describe clearly the plan through which you intend to accumulate it.

Sixth: Read your written statement aloud, twice daily, once just before retiring at night, and once after arising in the morning. AS YOU READ—SEE AND FEEL AND BELIEVE YOURSELF ALREADY IN

POSSESSION OF THE MONEY.

It is important that you follow the instructions described in these six steps. It is especially important that you observe, and follow the instructions in the sixth paragraph. You may complain that it is impossible for you to 'see yourself in possession of money' before you actually have it. Here is where a BURNING DESIRE will come to your aid. If you truly DESIRE money so keenly that your desire is an obsession, you will have no difficulty in convincing yourself that you will acquire it. The object is to want money, and to become so determined to have it that you CONVINCE yourself you will have it.

Only those who become 'money conscious' ever accumulate great riches. 'Money consciousness' means that the mind has become so thoroughly saturated with the DESIRE for money, that one can see one's self already in possession of it.

To the uninitiated, who has not been schooled in the working principles of the human mind, these instructions may appear impractical. It may be helpful, to all who fail to recognize the soundness of the six steps, to know that the information they convey, was received from Andrew Carnegie, who began as an ordinary laborer in the steel mills, but managed, despite his humble beginning, to make these principles yield him a fortune of considerably more than one hundred million dollars.

It may be of further help to know that the six steps here recommended were carefully scrutinized by the late Thomas A. Edison, who placed his stamp of approval upon them as being, not only the steps essential for the accumulation of money, but necessary for the attainment of *any definite goal.*

The steps call for no 'hard labor.' They call for no sacrifice.

They do not require one to become ridiculous, or credulous. To apply them calls for no great amount of education. But the successful application of these six steps does call for sufficient *imagination* to enable one to see, and to understand, that accumulation of money cannot be left to chance, good fortune, and luck. One must realize that all who have accumulated great fortunes, first did a certain amount of dreaming, hoping, wishing, DESIRING, and PLANNING *before* they acquired money.

You may as well know, right here, that you can never have riches in great quantities, UNLESS you can work yourself into a white heat of DESIRE for money, and actually BELIEVE you will possess it.

You may as well know, also that every great leader, from the dawn of civilization down to the present, was a dreamer. Christianity is the greatest potential power in the world today, because its founder was an intense dreamer who had the vision and the imagination to see realities in their mental and spiritual form before they had been transmuted into physical form.

If you do not see great riches in your imagination, you will never see them in your bank balance.

Never, in the history of America has there been so great an opportunity for practical dreamers as now exists. The six year economic collapse has reduced all men, substantially, to the same level. A new race is about to be run. The stakes represent huge fortunes which will be accumulated within the next ten years. The rules of the race have changed, because we now live in a CHANGED WORLD that definitely favors the masses, those who had but little or no opportunity to win under the conditions existing during the depression, when fear paralyzed growth and development.

We who are in this race for riches, should be encouraged to know that this changed world in which we live is demanding new ideas, new ways of doing things, new leaders, new inventions, new methods of teaching, new methods of marketing, new books, new literature, new features for the radio, new ideas for moving pictures. Back of all this demand for new and better things, there is one quality which one must possess to win, and that is DEFINITENESS OF PURPOSE, the knowledge of what one wants, and a burning DESIRE to possess it.

The business depression marked the death of one age, and the birth of another. This changed world requires practical dreamers who can, *and will* put their dreams into action. The practical dreamers have always been, and always will be the pattern-makers of civilization.

We who desire to accumulate riches, should remember the real leaders of the world always have been men who harnessed, and put into practical use, the intangible, unseen forces of unborn opportunity, and have converted those forces, [or impulses of thought], into sky-scrapers, cities, factories, airplanes, automobiles, and every form of convenience that makes life more pleasant.

Tolerance, and an open mind are practical necessities of the dreamer of today. Those who are afraid of new ideas are doomed before they start. Never has there been a time more favorable to pioneers than the present. True, there is no wild and woolly west to be conquered, as in the days of the Covered Wagon; but there is a vast business, financial, and industrial world to be remoulded and redirected along new and better lines.

In planning to acquire your share of the riches, let no one influence you to scorn the dreamer. To win the big stakes in this changed world, you must catch the spirit of the great pioneers of the past, whose dreams have given to civilization all that it has of value, the spirit which serves as the life-blood of our own country—your opportunity and mine, to develop and market our talents.

Let us not forget, Columbus dreamed of an Unknown world, staked his life on the existence of such a world, and discovered it!

Copernicus, the great astronomer, dreamed of a multiplicity of worlds, and revealed them! No one denounced him as 'impractical' *after* he had triumphed. Instead, the world worshipped at his shrine, thus proving once more that 'SUCCESS REQUIRES NO APOLOGIES, FAILURE PERMITS NO ALIBIS.'

If the thing you wish to do is right, and *you believe in it*, go ahead and do it! Put your dream across, and never mind what 'they' say if you meet with temporary defeat, for 'they,' perhaps, do not know that EVERY FAILURE BRINGS WITH IT THE SEED OF AN EQUIVALENT SUCCESS.

Henry Ford, poor and uneducated, dreamed of a horseless carriage, went to work with what tools he possessed, without waiting for opportunity to favor him, and now evidence of his dream belts the entire earth. He has put more wheels into operation than any man who ever lived, because he was not afraid to back his dreams.

Thomas Edison dreamed of a lamp that could be operated by electricity, began where he stood to put his dream into action, and despite more than ten thousand failures, he stood by that dream until he made it a physical reality. Practical dreamers DO NOT QUIT!

Whelan dreamed of a chain of cigar stores, transformed his dream into action, and now the United Cigar Stores occupy the best corners in America.

Lincoln dreamed of freedom for the black slaves, put his dream into action, and barely missed living to see a united North and South translate his dream into reality.

The Wright brothers dreamed of a machine that would fly through the air. Now one may see evidence all over the world, that they dreamed soundly.

Marconi dreamed of a system for harnessing the intangible forces of the ether. Evidence that he did not dream in vain, may be found in every wireless and radio in the world. Moreover, Marconi's dream brought the humblest cabin, and the most stately manor house side by side. It made the people of every nation on earth back-door neighbors. It gave the President of the United States a medium by which he may talk to all the people of America at one time, and on short notice. It may interest you to know that Marconi's 'friends' had him taken into custody, and examined in a psychopathic hospital, when he announced he had discovered a principle through which he could send messages through the air, without the aid of wires, or other direct physical means of communication. The dreamers of today fare better.

The world has become accustomed to new discoveries. Nay, it has shown a willingness to reward the dreamer who gives the world a new idea.

'The greatest achievement was, at first, and for a time, but a dream.'

'The oak sleeps in the acorn. The bird waits in the egg, and in the highest vision of the soul, a waking angel stirs. DREAMS ARE THE SEEDLINGS OF REALITY.'

Awake, arise, and assert yourself, you dreamers of the world.

Your star is now in the ascendency. The world depression brought the opportunity you have been waiting for. It taught people humility, tolerance, and open-mindedness.

The world is filled with an abundance of OPPORTUNITY which the dreamers of the past never knew.

A BURNING DESIRE TO BE, AND TO DO is the starting point from which the dreamer must take off. Dreams are not born of indifference, laziness, or lack of ambition.

The world no longer scoffs at the dreamer, nor calls him impractical. If you think it does, take a trip to Tennessee, and witness what a dreamer President has done in the way of harnessing, and using the great water power of America. A score of years ago, such a dream would have seemed like madness.

You have been disappointed, you have undergone defeat during the depression, you have felt the great heart within you crushed until it bled. Take courage, for these experiences have tempered the spiritual metal of which you are made—they are assets of incomparable value.

Remember, too, that all who succeed in life get off to a bad start, and pass through many heartbreaking struggles before they 'arrive.' The turning point in the lives of those who succeed, usually comes at the moment of some crisis, through which they are introduced to their 'other selves.'

John Bunyan wrote the Pilgrim's Progress, which is among the finest of all English literature, after he had been confined in prison and sorely punished, because of his views on the subject of religion.

O. Henry discovered the genius which slept within his brain, after he had met with great misfortune, and was confined in a prison cell, in Columbus, Ohio. Being FORCED, through misfortune, to become acquainted with his 'other self,' and to use his IMAGINATION, he discovered himself to be a great author instead of a miserable criminal and outcast. Strange and varied are the ways of life, and stranger still are the ways of Infinite Intelligence, through which men are sometimes forced to undergo all sorts of punishment before discovering their own brains, and their own capacity to create useful ideas through imagination.

Edison, the world's greatest inventor and scientist, was a 'tramp' telegraph operator, he failed innumerable times before he was driven, finally, to the discovery of the genius which slept within his brain.

Charles Dickens began by pasting labels on blacking pots. The tragedy of his first love penetrated the depths of his soul, and converted him into one of the world's truly great authors. That tragedy produced, first, David Copperfield, then a succession of other works that made this a richer and better world for all who read his books. Disappointment over love affairs, generally has the effect of driving men to drink, and women to ruin; and this, because most people never learn the art of transmuting their strongest emotions into dreams of a constructive nature.

Helen Keller became deaf, dumb, and blind shortly after birth. Despite her greatest misfortune, she has written her name indelibly in the pages of the history of the great. Her entire life has served as evidence that *no one ever is defeated until defeat has been accepted as a reality*.

Robert Burns was an illiterate country lad, he was cursed by poverty, and grew up to be a drunkard in the bargain. The world was made better for his having lived, because he clothed beautiful thoughts in poetry, and thereby plucked a thorn and planted a rose in its place.

Booker T. Washington was born in slavery, handicapped by race and color. Because he was tolerant, had an open mind at all times, on all subjects, and was a DREAMER, he left his impress for good on an entire race.

Beethoven was deaf, Milton was blind, but their names will last as long as time endures, because they dreamed and translated their dreams into organized thought.

Before passing to the next chapter, kindle anew in your mind the fire of hope, faith, courage, and tolerance. If you have these states of mind, and a working knowledge of the principles described, all else that you need will come to you, when you are READY for it. Let Emerson state the thought in these words, 'Every proverb, every book, every byword that belongs to thee for aid and comfort shall surely come home through open or winding passages. Every friend whom not thy fantastic will, but the great and tender soul in thee craveth, shall lock thee in his embrace.'

There is a difference between WISHING for a thing and being READY to receive it. No one is ready for a thing, until he believes he can acquire it. The state of mind must be BELIEF, not mere hope or wish. Open-mindedness is essential for belief. Closed minds do not inspire faith, courage, and belief.

Remember, no more effort is required to aim high in life, to demand abundance and prosperity, than is required to accept misery and poverty. A great poet has correctly stated this universal truth through these lines:

I bargained with Life for a penny,
And Life would pay no more,

However I begged at evening
When I counted my scanty store.

For Life is a just employer,
He gives you what you ask,
But once you have set the wages,
Why, you must bear the task.

I worked for a menial's hire,
Only to learn, dismayed,
That any wage I had asked of Life,
Life would have willingly paid.

DESIRE OUTWITS MOTHER NATURE

As a fitting climax to this chapter, I wish to introduce one of the most unusual persons I have ever known. I first saw him twenty-four years ago, a few minutes after he was born. He came into the world without any physical sign of ears, and the doctor admitted, when pressed for an opinion, that the child might be deaf, and mute for life.

I challenged the doctor's opinion. I had the right to do so, I was the child's father. I, too, reached a decision, and rendered an opinion, but I expressed the opinion silently, in the secrecy of my own heart. I decided that my son would hear and speak. Nature could send me a child without ears, but Nature *could not induce me to accept* the reality of the affliction.

In my own mind I knew that my son would hear and speak. How? I was sure there must be a way, and I knew I would find it. I thought of the words of the immortal Emerson, 'The whole course of things goes to teach us faith. We need only obey.

There is guidance for each of us, and by lowly listening, we shall hear *the right word.*'

The right word? DESIRE! More than anything else, I DESIRED that my son should not be a deaf mute. From that desire I never receded, not for a second.

Many years previously, I had written, 'Our only limitations are those we set up in our own minds.' For the first time, I wondered if that statement were true. Lying on the bed in front of me was a newly born child, without the natural equipment of hearing. Even though he might hear and speak, he was obviously disfigured for life. Surely, this was a limitation which that child had not set up in his own mind.

What could I do about it? Somehow I would find a way to transplant into that child's mind my own BURNING DESIRE for ways and means of conveying sound to his brain without the aid of ears.

As soon as the child was old enough to cooperate, I would fill his mind so completely with a BURNING DESIRE to hear, that Nature would, by methods of her own, translate it into physical reality.

All this thinking took place in my own mind, but I spoke of it to no one. Every day I renewed the pledge I had made to myself, not to accept a deaf mute for a son.

As he grew older, and began to take notice of things around him, we observed that he had a slight degree of hearing. When he reached the age when children usually begin talking, he made no attempt to speak, but we could tell by his actions that he could hear certain sounds slightly. That was all I wanted to know! I was convinced that if he could hear, even slightly, he might develop still greater hearing capacity. Then something happened which gave me hope. It came from an entirely unexpected source.

We bought a victrola. When the child heard the music for the first time, he went into ecstasies, and promptly appropriated the machine. He soon showed a preference for certain records, among them, 'It's a Long Way to Tipperary.' On one occasion, he played that piece over and over, for almost two hours, standing in front of the victrola, *with his teeth clamped on the edge of the case*. The significance of this self-formed habit of his did not become clear to us until years afterward, for we had never heard of the principle of 'bone conduction' of sound at that time.

Shortly after he appropriated the victrola, I discovered that he could hear me quite clearly when I spoke with my lips touching his mastoid bone, or at the base of the brain. These discoveries placed in my possession the necessary media by which I began to translate into reality my *Burning Desire* to help my son develop hearing and speech. By that time he was making stabs at speaking certain words. The outlook was far from encouraging, but DESIRE BACKED BY FAITH knows no such word as impossible.

Having determined that he could hear the sound of my voice plainly, I began, immediately, to transfer to his mind the desire to hear and speak. I soon discovered that the child enjoyed bedtime stories, so I went to work, creating stories designed to develop in him self-reliance, imagination, and a *keen desire to hear and to be normal.*

There was one story in particular, which I emphasized by giving it some new and dramatic coloring each time it was told. It was designed to plant in his mind the thought that his affliction was not a liability, but an asset of great value. Despite the fact that all the philosophy I had examined clearly indicated that EVERY ADVERSITY BRINGS WITH IT THE SEED OF AN EQUIVALENT ADVANTAGE, I must confess that I had not the slightest idea *how* this affliction could ever become an asset. However, I continued my practice of wrapping that philosophy in bedtime stories, hoping the time would come when he would find some plan by which his handicap could be made to serve some useful purpose. Reason told me plainly, that there was no adequate compensation for the lack of ears and natural hearing equipment. DESIRE backed by FAITH, pushed reason aside, and inspired me to carry on.

As I analyze the experience in retrospect, I can see now, that my son's *faith in me* had much to do with the astounding results. He did not question anything I told him. I sold him the idea that he had a distinct *advantage* over his older brother, and that this advantage would reflect itself in many ways. For example, the teachers in school would observe that he had no ears, and, because of this, they would show him special attention and treat him with extraordinary kindness. They always did. His mother saw to that, by visiting the teachers and arranging with them to give the child the extra attention necessary. I sold him the idea, too, that when he became old enough to sell newspapers, (his older brother had already become a newspaper merchant), he would have a big advantage over his brother, for the reason that people would pay him extra money for his wares, because they could see that he was a bright, industrious boy, despite the fact he had no ears.

We could notice that, gradually, the child's hearing was improving. Moreover, he had not the slightest tendency to be self-conscious, because of his affliction. When he was about seven, he showed the first evidence that our method of servicing his mind was bearing fruit. For several months he begged for the privilege of selling newspapers, but his mother would not give her consent. She was afraid that his deafness made it unsafe for him to go on the street alone.

Finally, he took matters in his own hands. One afternoon, when he was left at home with the servants, he climbed through the kitchen window, shinnied to the ground, and set out on his own. He borrowed six cents in capital from the neighborhood shoemaker, invested it in papers, sold out, reinvested, and kept repeating until late in the evening. After balancing his accounts, and paying back the six cents he had borrowed from his banker, he had a net profit of forty-two cents. When we got home that night, we found him in bed asleep, with the money tightly clenched in his hand.

His mother opened his hand, removed the coins, and cried. Of all things! Crying over her son's first victory seemed so inappropriate. My reaction was the reverse. I laughed heartily, for I knew that my endeavor to plant in the child's mind an attitude of faith in himself had been successful.

His mother saw, in his first business venture, a little deaf boy who had gone out in the streets and risked his life to earn money. I saw a brave, ambitious, self-reliant little business man whose stock in himself had been increased a hundred percent, because he had gone into business on his own initiative, and had won. The transaction pleased me, because I knew that he had given evidence of a trait of resourcefulness that would go with him all through life. Later events proved this to be true. When his older brother wanted something, he would lie down on the floor, kick his feet in the air, cry for it—and get it. When the 'little deaf boy' wanted something, he would plan a way to earn the money, then buy it for himself. He still follows that plan!

Truly, my own son has taught me that handicaps can be converted into stepping stones on which one may climb toward some worthy goal, unless they are accepted as obstacles, and used as alibis.

The little deaf boy went through the grades, high school, and college without being able to hear his teachers, excepting when they shouted loudly, at close range. He did not go to a school for the deaf.

WE WOULD NOT PERMIT HIM TO LEARN THE SIGN LANGUAGE.

We were determined that he should live a normal life, and associate with normal children, and we stood by that decision, although it cost us many heated debates with school officials.

While he was in high school, he tried an electrical hearing aid, but it was of no value to him; due, we believed, to a condition that was disclosed when the child was six, by Dr J. Gordon Wilson, of Chicago, when he operated on one side of the boy's head, and discovered that there was no sign of natural hearing equipment.

During his last week in college, (eighteen years after the operation), something happened which marked the most important turning-point of his life. Through what seemed to be mere chance, he came into possession of another electrical hearing device, which was sent to him on trial. He was slow about testing it, due to his disappointment with a similar device. Finally he picked the instrument up, and more or less carelessly, placed it on his head, hooked up the battery, and lo! as if by a stroke of magic, his lifelong DESIRE FOR NORMAL HEARING BECAME A REALITY! For the first time in his life he heard practically as well as any person with normal hearing. 'God moves in mysterious ways, His wonders to perform.'

Overjoyed because of the Changed World which had been brought to him through his hearing device, he rushed to the telephone, called his mother, and heard her voice perfectly. The next day he plainly heard the voices of his professors in class, for the first time in his life! Previously he could hear them only when they shouted, at short range. He heard the radio. He *heard* the talking pictures. For the first time in his life, he could converse freely with other people, without the necessity of their having to speak loudly. Truly, he had come into possession of a Changed World. We had refused to accept Nature's error, and, by PERSISTENT DESIRE, we had induced Nature to correct that error, through the only practical means available.

DESIRE had commenced to pay dividends, but the victory was not yet complete. The boy still had to find a definite and practical way to convert his handicap into an *equivalent asset.*

Hardly realizing the significance of what had already been accomplished, but intoxicated with the joy of his newly discovered world of sound, he wrote a letter to the manufacturer of the hearing-aid, enthusiastically describing his experience. Something in his letter; something, perhaps which was not written on the lines, but back of them; caused the company to invite him to New York. When be arrived, he was escorted through the factory, and while talking with the Chief Engineer, telling him about his changed world, a hunch, an idea, or an inspiration—call it what you wish—flashed into his mind. It was this *impulse of thought* which converted his affliction into an asset, destined to pay dividends in both money and happiness to thousands for all time to come.

The sum and substance of that impulse of thought was this: It occurred to him that he might be of help to the millions of deafened people who go through life without the benefit of hearing devices, if he could find a way to tell them the story of his Changed World. Then and there, he reached a decision to devote the remainder of his life to rendering useful service to the hard of hearing.

For an entire month, he carried on an intensive research, during which he analyzed the entire marketing system of the manufacturer of the hearing device, and created ways and means of communicating with the hard of hearing all over the world for the purpose of sharing with them his newly discovered 'Changed World.' When this was done, he put in writing a two-year plan, based upon his findings. When he presented the plan to the company, he was instantly given a position, for the purpose of carrying out his ambition.

Little did he dream, when he went to work, that he was destined to bring hope and practical relief to thousands of deafened people who, without his help, would have been doomed forever to deaf mutism.

Shortly after he became associated with the manufacturer of his hearing aid, he invited me to attend a class conducted by his company, for the purpose of teaching deaf mutes to hear, and to speak. I had never heard of such a form of education, therefore I visited the class, skeptical but hopeful that my time would not be entirely wasted. Here I saw a demonstration which gave me a greatly enlarged vision of what I had done to arouse and keep alive in my son's mind the DESIRE for normal hearing. I saw deaf mutes actually being taught to hear and to speak, through application of the self-same principle I had used, more than twenty years previously, in saving my son from deaf mutism.

Thus, through some strange turn of the Wheel of Fate, my son, Blair, and I have been destined to aid in correcting deaf mutism for those as yet unborn, because we are the only living human beings, as far as I know, who have established definitely the fact that deaf mutism can be corrected to the extent of restoring to normal life those who suffer with this affliction. It has been done for one; it will be done for others.

There is no doubt in my mind that Blair would have been a deaf mute all his life, if his mother and I had not managed to shape his mind as we did. The doctor who attended at his birth told us, confidentially, the child might never hear or speak. A few weeks ago, Dr Irving Voorhees, a noted specialist on such cases, examined Blair very thoroughly. He was astounded when he learned how well my son now hears, and speaks, and said his examination indicated that 'theoretically, the boy should not be able to hear at all.' But the lad does hear, despite the fact that X-ray pictures show there is no opening in the skull, whatsoever, from where his ears should be to the brain.

When I planted in his mind the DESIRE to hear and talk, and live as a normal person, there went with that impulse some strange influence which caused Nature to become bridge-builder, and span the gulf of silence between his brain and the outer world, by some means which the keenest medical specialists have not been able to interpret. It would be sacrilege for me to even conjecture as to how Nature performed this miracle. It would be unforgivable if I neglected to tell the world as much as I know of the humble part I assumed in the strange experience. It is my duty, and a privilege to say I believe, and not without reason, that nothing is impossible to the person who backs DESIRE with enduring FAITH.

Verily, a BURNING DESIRE has devious ways of transmuting itself into its physical equivalent. Blair DESIRED normal hearing; now he has it! He was born with a handicap which might easily have sent one with a less defined DESIRE to the street with a bundle of pencils and a tin cup. That handicap now promises to serve as the medium by which he will render useful service to many millions of hard of hearing, also, to give him useful employment at adequate financial compensation the remainder of his life.

The little 'white lies' I planted in his mind when he was a child, by leading him to BELIEVE his affliction would become a great asset, which he could capitalize, has justified itself. Verily, there is nothing, right or wrong, which BELIEF, plus BURNING DESIRE, cannot make real. These qualities are free to everyone.

In all my experience in dealing with men and women who had personal problems, I never handled a single case which more definitely demonstrates the power of DESIRE. Authors sometimes make the mistake of writing of subjects of which they have but superficial, or very elementary knowledge. It has been my good fortune to have had the privilege of testing the soundness of the POWER OF DESIRE, through the affliction of my own son. Perhaps it was providential that the experience came as it did, for surely no one is better prepared than he, to serve as an example of what happens when DESIRE is put to the test. *If Mother Nature bends to the will of desire, is it logical that mere men can defeat a burning desire?*

Strange and imponderable is the power of the human mind! We do not understand the method by which it uses every circumstance, every individual, every physical thing within its reach, as a means of transmuting DESIRE into its physical counterpart. Perhaps science will uncover this secret.

I planted in my son's mind the DESIRE to hear and to speak as any normal person hears and speaks. That DESIRE has now become a reality. I planted in his mind the DESIRE to convert his greatest handicap into his greatest asset. That DESIRE has been realized. The modus operandi by which this astounding result was achieved is not hard to describe. It consisted of three very definite facts; first, I MIXED FAITH with the DESIRE for normal hearing, which I passed on to my son. Second, I communicated my desire to him in every conceivable way available, through persistent, continuous effort, over a period of years. Third, HE BELIEVED ME!

As this chapter was being completed, news came of the death of Mme.

Schuman-Heink. One short paragraph in the news dispatch gives the clue to this unusual woman's stupendous success as a singer. I quote the paragraph, because the clue it contains is none other than DESIRE.

Early in her career, Mme. Schuman-Heink visited the director of the Vienna Court Opera, to have him test her voice. But, he did not test it. After taking one look at the awkward and poorly dressed girl, he exclaimed, none too gently,

'With such a face, and with no personality at all, how can you ever expect to succeed in opera? My good child, give up the idea. Buy a sewing machine, and go to work. YOU CAN NEVER BE A SINGER.'

Never is a long time! The director of the Vienna Court Opera knew much about the technique of singing. He knew little about the power of desire, when it assumes the proportion of an obsession. If he had known more of that power, he would not have made the mistake of condemning genius without giving it an opportunity.

Several years ago, one of my business associates became ill. He became worse as time went on, and finally was taken to the hospital for an operation. Just before he was wheeled into the operating room, I took a look at him, and wondered how anyone as thin and emaciated as he, could possibly go through a major operation successfully. The doctor warned me that there was little if any chance of my ever seeing him alive again. But that was the DOCTOR's OPINION. It was not the opinion of the patient. Just before he was wheeled away, he whispered feebly, 'Do not be disturbed, Chief, I will be out of here in a few days.' The attending nurse looked at me with pity. But the patient did come through safely. After it was all over, his physician said, 'Nothing but his own desire to live saved him. He never would have pulled through if he had not refused to accept the possibility of death.'

I believe in the power of DESIRE backed by FAITH, because I have seen this power lift men from lowly beginnings to places of power and wealth; I have seen it rob the grave of its victims; I have seen it serve as the medium by which men staged a comeback after having been defeated in a hundred different ways; I have seen it provide my own son with a normal, happy, successful life, despite Nature's having sent him into the world without ears.

How can one harness and use the power of DESIRE? This has been answered through this, and the subsequent chapters of this book. This message is going out to the world at the end of the longest, and perhaps, the most devastating depression America has ever known. It is reasonable to presume that the message may come to the attention of many who have been wounded by the depression, those who have lost their fortunes, others who have lost their positions, and great numbers who must reorganize their plans and stage a comeback. To all these I wish to convey the thought that all achievement, no matter what may be its nature, or its purpose, must begin with an intense, BURNING DESIRE for something definite.

Through some strange and powerful principle of 'mental chemistry' which she has never divulged, Nature wraps up in the impulse of STRONG DESIRE 'that something' which recognizes no such word as impossible, and accepts no such reality as failure.

2

ORGANIZED PLANNING
The Crystallization of Desire into Action

You have learned that everything man creates or acquires, begins in the form of DESIRE, that desire is taken on the first lap of its journey, from the abstract to the concrete, into the workshop of the IMAGINATION, where PLANS for its transition are created and organized.

In Chapter two, you were instructed to take six definite, practical steps, as your first move in translating the desire for money into its monetary equivalent. One of these steps is the formation of a DEFINITE, practical plan, or plans, through which this transformation may be made. You will now be instructed how to build plans which will be practical, viz:

(a) Ally yourself with a group of as many people as you may need for the creation, and carrying out of your plan, or plans for the accumulation of money—making use of the 'Master Mind' principle described in a later chapter. (Compliance with this instruction is absolutely essential. Do not neglect it.)

(b) Before forming your 'Master Mind' alliance, decide what advantages, and benefits, you may offer the individual members of your group, in return for their cooperation. No one will work indefinitely without some form of compensation. No intelligent person will either request or expect another to work without adequate compensation, although this may not always be in the form of money.

(c) Arrange to meet with the members of your 'Master Mind' group at least twice a week, and more often if possible, until you have jointly perfected the necessary plan, or plans for the accumulation of money.

(d) Maintain PERFECT HARMONY between yourself and every member of your 'Master Mind' group. If you fail to carry out this instruction to the letter, you may expect to meet with failure. The 'Master Mind' principle cannot obtain where PERFECT HARMONY does not prevail.

Keep in mind these facts:

First. You are engaged in an undertaking of major importance to you. To be sure of success, you must have plans which are faultless.

Second. You must have the advantage of the experience, education, native ability and imagination of other minds. This is in harmony with the methods followed by every person who has accumulated a great fortune.

No individual has sufficient experience, education, native ability, and knowledge to insure the accumulation of a great fortune, without the cooperation of other people. Every plan you adopt, in your endeavor to accumulate wealth, should be the joint creation of yourself and every other member of your 'Master Mind' group. You may originate your own plans, either in whole or in part, but SEE THAT THOSE PLANS ARE CHECKED, AND APPROVED BY THE MEMBERS OF YOUR 'MASTER MIND' ALLIANCE.

If the first plan which you adopt does not work successfully, replace it with a new plan, if this new plan fails to work, replace it, in turn with still another, and so on, until you find a plan which DOES WORK. Right here is the point at which the majority of men meet with failure, because of their lack of PERSISTENCE in creating new plans to take the place of those which fail.

The most intelligent man living cannot succeed in accumulating money—nor in any other undertaking—without plans which are practical and workable. Just keep this fact in mind, and remember when your plans fail, that temporary defeat is not permanent failure. It may only mean that your plans have not been sound. Build other plans. Start all over again.

Thomas A. Edison 'failed' ten thousand times before he perfected the incandescent electric light bulb. That is—he met with *temporary defeat* ten thousand times, before his efforts were crowned with success.

Temporary defeat should mean only one thing, the certain knowledge that there is something wrong with your plan. Millions of men go through life in misery and poverty, because they lack a sound plan through which to accumulate a fortune.

Henry Ford accumulated a fortune, not because of his superior mind, but because he adopted and followed a PLAN which proved to be sound. A thousand men could be pointed out, each with a better education than Ford's, yet each of whom lives in poverty, because he does not possess the RIGHT plan for the accumulation of money.

Your achievement can be no greater than your PLANS are sound. That may seem to be an axiomatic statement, but it is true. Samuel Insull lost his fortune of over one hundred million dollars. The Insull fortune was built on plans which were sound. The business depression forced Mr Insull to CHANGE HIS PLANS; and the CHANGE brought 'temporary defeat,' because his new plans were NOT SOUND. Mr Insull is now an old man, he may, consequently, accept 'failure' instead of 'temporary defeat,' but if his experience turns out to be FAILURE, it will be for the reason that he lacks the fire of PERSISTENCE to rebuild his plans.

No man is ever whipped, until he QUITS—in *his own mind.*

This fact will be repeated many times, because it is so easy to 'take the count' at the first sign of defeat.

James J. Hill met with temporary defeat when he first endeavored to raise the necessary capital to build a railroad from the East to the West, but he, too turned defeat into victory *through new plans.*

Henry Ford met with temporary defeat, not only at the beginning of his automobile career, but after he had gone far toward the top. He created new plans, and went marching on to financial victory.

We see men who have accumulated great fortunes, but we often recognize only their triumph, overlooking the temporary defeats which they had to surmount before 'arriving.'

NO FOLLOWER OF THIS PHILOSOPHY CAN REASONABLY EXPECT TO ACCUMULATE A FORTUNE

WITHOUT EXPERIENCING 'TEMPORARY DEFEAT.' When defeat comes, accept it as a signal that your plans are not sound, rebuild those plans, and set sail once more toward your coveted goal. If you give up before your goal has been reached, you are a 'quitter.'

A QUITTER NEVER WINS—AND—A WINNER NEVER QUITS.

Lift this sentence out, write it on a piece of paper in letters an inch high, and place it where you will see it every night before you go to sleep, and every morning before you go to work.

When you begin to select members for your 'Master Mind' group, endeavor to select those who do not take defeat seriously.

Some people foolishly believe that only MONEY can make money. This is not true! DESIRE, transmuted into its monetary equivalent, through the principles laid down here, is the agency through which money is 'made.' Money, of itself, is nothing but inert matter. It cannot move, think, or talk, but it can 'hear' when a man who DESIRES it, calls it to come!

PLANNING THE SALE OF SERVICES

The remainder of this chapter has been given over to a description of ways and means of marketing personal services. The information here conveyed will be of practical help to any person having any form of personal services to market, but it will be of priceless benefit to those who aspire to leadership in their chosen occupations.

Intelligent planning is essential for success in any undertaking designed to accumulate riches. Here will be found detailed instructions to those who must begin the accumulation of riches by selling personal services.

It should be encouraging to know that practically all the great fortunes began in the form of compensation for personal services, or from the sale of IDEAS. What else, except ideas and personal services, would one not possessed of property have to give in return for riches?

Broadly speaking, there are two types of people in the world. One type is known as LEADERS, and the other as FOLLOWERS. Decide at the outset whether you intend to become a leader in your chosen calling, or remain a follower. The difference in compensation is vast. The follower cannot reasonably expect the compensation to which a leader is entitled, although many followers make the mistake of expecting such pay.

It is no disgrace to be a follower. On the other hand, it is no credit to remain a follower. Most great leaders began in the capacity of followers. They became great leaders because they were INTELLIGENT FOLLOWERS. With few exceptions, the man who cannot follow a leader intelligently, cannot become an efficient leader. The man who can follow a leader most efficiently, is usually the man who develops into leadership most rapidly. An intelligent follower has many advantages, among them the OPPORTUNITY TO ACQUIRE KNOWLEDGE FROM HIS LEADER.

THE MAJOR ATTRIBUTES OF LEADERSHIP

The following are important factors of leadership:—

1. UNWAVERING COURAGE based upon knowledge of self, and of one's occupation. No follower wishes to be

dominated by a leader who lacks self- confidence and courage. No intelligent follower will be dominated by such a leader very long.

2. SELF-CONTROL. The man who cannot control himself, can never control others. Self-control sets a mighty example for one's followers, which the more intelligent will emulate.
3. A KEEN SENSE OF JUSTICE. Without a sense of fairness and justice, no leader can command and retain the respect of his followers.
4. DEFINITENESS OF DECISION. The man who wavers in his decisions, shows that he is not sure of himself. He cannot lead others successfully.
5. DEFINITENESS OF PLANS. The successful leader must plan his work, and *work his plan.* A leader who moves by guesswork, without practical, definite plans, is comparable to a ship without a rudder. Sooner or later he will land on the rocks.
6. THE HABIT OF DOING MORE THAN PAID FOR. One of the penalties of leadership is the necessity of willingness, upon the part of the leader, to do more than he requires of his followers.
7. A PLEASING PERSONALITY. No slovenly, careless person can become a successful leader. Leadership calls for respect. Followers will not respect a leader who does not grade high on all of the factors of a Pleasing Personality.
8. SYMPATHY AND UNDERSTANDING. The successful leader must be in sympathy with his followers. Moreover, he must understand them and their problems.
9. MASTERY OF DETAIL. Successful leadership calls for mastery of details of the leader's position.

10. WILLINGNESS TO ASSUME FULL RESPONSIBILITY. The successful leader must be willing to assume responsibility for the mistakes and the shortcomings of his followers. If he tries to shift this responsibility, he will not remain the leader. If one of his followers makes a mistake, and shows himself incompetent, the leader must consider that it is he who failed.
11. COOPERATION. The successful leader must understand, and *apply* the principle of cooperative effort and be able to induce his followers to do the same. Leadership calls for POWER, and power calls for COOPERATION.

There are two forms of Leadership. The first, and by far the most effective, is LEADERSHIP BY CONSENT of, and with the sympathy of the followers. The second is LEADERSHIP BY FORCE, without the consent and sympathy of the followers.

History is filled with evidences that Leadership by Force cannot endure. The downfall and disappearance of 'Dictators' and kings is significant. It means that people will not follow forced leadership indefinitely.

The world has just entered a new era of relationship between leaders and followers, which very clearly calls for new leaders, and a new brand of leadership in business and industry. Those who belong to the old school of leadership-by-force, must acquire an understanding of the new brand of leadership (cooperation) or be relegated to the rank and file of the followers. There is no other way out for them.

The relationship of employer and employee, or of leader and follower, in the future, will be one of mutual cooperation, based upon an equitable division of the profits of business. In the future, the relationship of employer and employee will be more like a partnership than it has been in the past.

Napoleon, Kaiser Wilhelm of Germany, the Czar of Russia, and the King of Spain were examples of leadership by force. Their leadership passed. Without much difficulty, one might point to the prototypes of these ex-leaders, among the business, financial, and labor leaders of America who have been dethroned or slated to go. *Leadership-by-consent* of the followers is the only brand which can endure!

Men may follow the forced leadership temporarily, but they will not do so willingly.

The new brand of LEADERSHIP will embrace the eleven factors of leadership, described in this chapter, as well as some other factors. The man who makes these the basis of his leadership, will find abundant opportunity to lead in any walk of life. The depression was prolonged, largely, because the world lacked LEADERSHIP of the new brand. At the end of the depression, the demand for leaders who are competent to apply the new methods of leadership has greatly exceeded the supply. Some of the old type of leaders will reform and adapt themselves to the new brand of leadership, but generally speaking, the world will have to look for new timber for its leadership. *This necessity may be your OPPORTUNITY!*

THE TEN MAJOR CAUSES OF FAILURE IN LEADERSHIP

We come now to the major faults of leaders who fail, because it is just as essential to know WHAT NOT TO DO as it is to know what to do.

1. INABILITY TO ORGANIZE DETAILS. Efficient leadership calls for ability to organize and to master details. No genuine leader is ever 'too busy' to do anything which may be required of him in his capacity as leader. When a man, whether he is a leader or follower, admits that he is 'too busy' to change his plans, or to give attention to any emergency, he admits his inefficiency. The successful leader must be the master of all details connected with his position. That means, of course, that he must acquire the habit of relegating details to capable lieutenants.
2. UNWILLINGNESS TO RENDER HUMBLE SERVICE. Truly great leaders are willing, when occasion demands, to perform any sort of labor which they would ask another to perform. 'The greatest among ye shall be the servant of all' is a truth which all able leaders observe and respect.
3. EXPECTATION OF PAY FOR WHAT THEY 'KNOW' INSTEAD OF WHAT THEY *DO* WITH THAT WHICH THEY KNOW. The world does not pay men for that which they 'know.' It pays them for what they DO, or induce others to do.
4. FEAR OF COMPETITION FROM FOLLOWERS. The leader who fears that one of his followers may take his position is practically sure to realize that fear sooner or later. The able leader trains understudies to whom he may delegate, at will, any of the details of his position. Only in this way may a leader multiply himself and prepare himself to be at many places, and give attention to many things at one time. It is an eternal truth that men receive more pay for their ABILITY TO GET OTHERS TO PERFORM, than they could possibly earn by their own efforts. An

efficient leader may, through his knowledge of his job and the magnetism of his personality, greatly increase the efficiency of others, and induce them to render more service and better service than they could render without his aid.

5. LACK OF IMAGINATION. Without imagination, the leader is incapable of meeting emergencies, and of creating plans by which to guide his followers efficiently.
6. SELFISHNESS. The leader who claims all the honor for the work of his followers, is sure to be met by resentment. The really great leader CLAIMS NONE OF THE HONORS. He is contented to see the honors, when there are any, go to his followers, because he knows that most men will work harder for commendation and recognition than they will for money alone.
7. INTEMPERANCE. Followers do not respect an intemperate leader. Moreover, intemperance in any of its various forms, destroys the endurance and the vitality of all who indulge in it.
8. DISLOYALTY. Perhaps this should have come at the head of the list. The leader who is not loyal to his trust, and to his associates, those above him, and those below him, cannot long maintain his leadership. Disloyalty marks one as being less than the dust of the earth, and brings down on one's head the contempt he deserves. Lack of loyalty is one of the major causes of failure in every walk of life.
9. EMPHASIS OF THE 'AUTHORITY' OF LEADERSHIP. The efficient leader leads by encouraging, and not by trying to instil fear in the hearts of his followers. The leader who tries to impress his followers with his 'authority' comes within the category of leadership through FORCE. If

a leader is a REAL LEADER, he will have no need to advertise that fact except by his conduct—his sympathy, understanding, fairness, and a demonstration that he knows his job.

10. EMPHASIS OF TITLE. The competent leader requires no 'title' to give him the respect of his followers. The man who makes too much over his title generally has little else to emphasize. The doors to the office of the real leader are open to all who wish to enter, and his working quarters are free from formality or ostentation.

These are among the more common of the causes of failure in leadership. Any one of these faults is sufficient to induce failure. Study the list carefully if you aspire to leadership, and make sure that you are free of these faults.

SOME FERTILE FIELDS IN WHICH 'NEW LEADERSHIP' WILL BE REQUIRED

Before leaving this chapter, your attention is called to a few of the fertile fields in which there has been a decline of leadership, and in which the new type of leader may find an abundance of OPPORTUNITY.

First: In the field of politics there is a most insistent demand for new leaders; a demand which indicates nothing less than an emergency. The majority of politicians have, seemingly, become high-grade, legalized racketeers. They have increased taxes and debauched the machinery of industry and business until the people can no longer stand the burden.

Second: The banking business is undergoing a reform. The leaders in this field have almost entirely lost the confidence of the public. Already the bankers have sensed the need of reform, and they have begun it.

Third: Industry calls for new leaders. The old type of leaders thought and moved in terms of dividends instead of thinking and moving in terms of human equations! The future leader in industry, to endure, must regard himself as a quasi-public official whose duty it is to manage his trust in such a way that it will work hardship on no individual, or group of individuals. Exploitation of working men is a thing of the past. Let the man who aspires to leadership in the field of business, industry, and labor remember this.

Fourth: The religious leader of the future will be forced to give more attention to the temporal needs of his followers, in the solution of their economic and personal problems of the present, and less attention to the dead past, and the yet unborn future.

Fifth: In the professions of law, medicine, and education, a new brand of leadership, and to some extent, new leaders will become a necessity. This is especially true in the field of education. The leader in that field must, in the future, find ways and means of teaching people HOW TO APPLY the knowledge they receive in school. He must deal more with PRACTICE and less with THEORY.

Sixth: New leaders will be required in the field of

Journalism. Newspapers of the future, to be conducted successfully, must be divorced from 'special privilege' and relieved from the subsidy of advertising. They must cease to be organs of propaganda for the interests which patronize their advertising columns. The type of newspaper which publishes scandal and lewd pictures will eventually go the way of all forces which debauch the human mind.

These are but a few of the fields in which opportunities for new leaders and a new brand of leadership are now available. The world is undergoing a rapid change. This means that the media through which the changes in human habits are promoted, must be adapted to the changes. The media here described, are the ones which, more than any others, determine the trend of civilization.

WHEN AND HOW TO APPLY FOR A POSITION

The information described here is the net result of many years of experience during which thousands of men and women were helped to market their services effectively. It can, therefore, be relied upon as sound and practical.

MEDIA THROUGH WHICH SERVICES MAY BE MARKETED

Experience has proved that the following media offer the most direct and effective methods of bringing the buyer and seller of personal services together.

1. EMPLOYMENT BUREAUS. Care must be taken to select only reputable bureaus, the management of which can show adequate records of achievement of satisfactory results. There are comparatively few such bureaus.
2. ADVERTISING in newspapers, trade journals, magazines, and radio. Classified advertising may usually be relied upon to produce satisfactory results in the case of those who apply for clerical or ordinary salaried positions. Display advertising is more desirable in the case of those who seek executive connections, the copy to appear in the section of the paper which is most apt to come to the attention of the class of employer being sought. The copy should be prepared by an expert, who understands how to inject sufficient selling qualities to produce replies.
3. PERSONAL LETTERS OF APPLICATION, directed to particular firms or individuals most apt to need such services as are being offered. Letters should be *neatly typed*, ALWAYS, and signed by hand. With the letter, should be sent a complete 'brief' or outline of the applicant's qualifications. Both the letter of application and the brief of experience or qualifications should be prepared by an expert. (See instructions as to information to be supplied).
4. APPLICATION THROUGH PERSONAL ACQUAINTANCES. When possible, the applicant should endeavor to approach prospective employers through some mutual acquaintance. This method of approach is particularly advantageous in the case of those who seek executive connections and do not wish to appear to be 'peddling' themselves.
5. APPLICATION IN PERSON. In some instances, it may be

more effective if the applicant offers personally, his services to prospective employers, in which event a complete written statement of qualifications for the position should be presented, for the reason that prospective employers often wish to discuss with associates, one's record.

INFORMATION TO BE SUPPLIED IN A WRITTEN 'BRIEF'

This brief should be prepared as carefully as a lawyer would prepare the brief of a case to be tried m court. Unless the applicant is experienced in the preparation of such briefs, an expert should be consulted, and his services enlisted for this purpose. Successful merchants employ men and women who understand the art and the psychology of advertising to present the merits of their merchandise. One who has personal services for sale should do the same. The following information should appear in the brief:

1. *Education.* State briefly, but definitely, what schooling you have had, and in what subjects you specialized in school, giving the reasons for that specialization.
2. *Experience.* If you have had experience in connection with positions similar to the one you seek, describe it fully, state names and addresses of former employers. Be sure to bring out clearly any special experience you may have had which would equip you to fill the position you seek.
3. *References.* Practically every business firm desires to know all about the previous records, antecedents, etc., of prospective employees who seek positions of responsibility. Attach to

your brief photostatic copies of letters from:

a. Former employers
b. Teachers under whom you studied
c. Prominent people whose judgement may be relied upon.

4. *Photograph of self.* Attach to your brief a recent, unmounted photograph of yourself.
5. *Apply for a specific position.* Avoid application for a position without describing EXACTLY what particular position you seek. Never apply for 'just a position.' That indicates you lack specialized qualifications.
6. *State your qualifications* for the particular position for which you apply. Give full details as to the reason you believe you are qualified for the particular position you seek. This is THE APPLICATION. It will determine, more than anything else, what consideration you receive.
7. *Offer to go to work on probation.* In the majority of instances if you are determined to have the position for which you apply, it will be most effective if you offer to work for a week, or a month, or for a sufficient length of time to enable your prospective employer to judge your value WITHOUT PAY. This may appear to be a radical suggestion, but experience has proved that it seldom fails to win at least a trial. If you are SURE OF YOUR QUALIFICATIONS, a trial is all you need. Incidentally, such an offer indicates that you have confidence in your ability to fill the position you seek. It is most convincing. If your offer is accepted, and you make good, more than likely you will be paid for your 'probation' period. Make clear the fact that your offer is based upon:
   a. Your confidence in your ability to fill the position.
   b. Your confidence in your prospective employer's decision

to employ you after trial.

c. Your DETERMINATION to have the position you seek.

8. *Knowledge of your prospective employer's business.* Before applying for a position, do sufficient research in connection with the business to familiarize yourself thoroughly with that business, and indicate in your brief the knowledge you have acquired in this field. This will be impressive, as it will indicate that you have imagination, and a real interest in the position you seek.

Remember that it is not the lawyer who knows the most law, but the one who best prepares his case, who wins. If your 'case' is properly prepared and presented, your victory will have been more than half won at the outset.

Do not be afraid of making your brief too long. Employers are just as much interested in purchasing the services of well-qualified applicants as you are in securing employment. In fact, the success of most successful employers is due, in the main, to their ability to select well-qualified lieutenants. They want all the information available.

Remember another thing; neatness in the preparation of your brief will indicate that you are a painstaking person. I have helped to prepare briefs for clients which were so striking and out of the ordinary that they resulted in the employment of the applicant without a personal interview.

When your brief has been completed, have it neatly bound by an experienced binder, and lettered by an artist, or printer similar to the following:

BRIEF OF THE QUALIFICATIONS OF
Robert K. Smith
APPLYING FOR THE POSITION OF
Private Secretary to The President of
THE BLANK COMPANY, Inc.

Change names each time brief is shown.

This personal touch is sure to command attention. Have your brief neatly typed or mimeographed on the finest paper you can obtain, and bound with a heavy paper of the book-cover variety, the binder to be changed, and the proper firm name to be inserted if it is to be shown to more than one company. Your photograph should be pasted on one of the pages of your brief. Follow these instructions to the letter, improving upon them wherever your imagination suggests.

Successful salesmen groom themselves with care. They understand that first impressions are lasting. Your brief is your salesman. Give it a good suit of clothes, so it will stand out in bold contrast to anything your prospective employer ever saw, in the way of an application for a position. If the position you seek is worth having, it is worth going after with care. Moreover, if you sell yourself to an employer in a manner that impresses him with your individuality, you probably will receive more money for your services from the very start, than you would if you applied for employment in the usual conventional way.

If you seek employment through an advertising agency, or an employment agency, have the agent use copies of your brief in marketing your services. This will help to gain preference for you, both with the agent, and the prospective employers.

HOW TO GET THE EXACT POSITION YOU DESIRE

Everyone enjoys doing the kind of work for which he is best suited. An artist loves to work with paints, a craftsman with his hands, a writer loves to write. Those with less definite talents have their preferences for certain fields of business and industry. If America does anything well, it offers a full range of occupations, tilling the soil, manufacturing, marketing, and the professions.

First: Decide EXACTLY what kind of a job you want. If the job doesn't already exist, perhaps you can create it.

Second: Choose the company, or individual for whom you wish to work.

Third: Study your prospective employer, as to policies, personnel, and chances of advancement.

Fourth: By analysis of yourself, your talents and capabilities, figure WHAT YOU CAN OFFER, and plan ways and means of giving advantages, services, developments, ideas that *you believe* you can successfully deliver.

Fifth: Forget about 'a job.' Forget whether or not there is an opening.

Forget the usual routine of 'have you got a job for me?' Concentrate on what *you can give.*

Sixth: Once you have your plan in mind, arrange with an experienced writer to put it on paper in neat form, and in full detail.

Seventh: Present it to the *proper person with authority* and he will do the rest. Every company is looking for men who can give something of value, whether it be ideas, services, or 'connections.' Every company has room for the man who has a definite plan of action which is to the advantage of that company.

This line of procedure may take a few days or weeks of extra time, but the difference in income, in advancement, and in gaining recognition will save years of hard work at small pay. It has many advantages, the main one being that it will often save from one to five years of time in reaching a chosen goal.

Every person who starts, or 'gets in' half way up the ladder, does so by deliberate and careful planning (excepting, of course, the Boss' son).

THE NEW WAY OF MARKETING SERVICES 'JOBS' ARE NOW 'PARTNERSHIPS'

Men and women who market their services to best advantage in the future, must recognize the stupendous change which has taken place in connection with the relationship between employer and employee.

In the future, the 'Golden Rule,' and not the 'Rule of Gold' will be the dominating factor in the marketing of merchandise as well as personal services. The future relationship between employers and their employees will be more in the nature of a partnership consisting of:

a. The employer
b. The employee
c. The public they serve

This new way of marketing personal services is called new for many reasons, first, both the employer and the employee of the future will be considered as fellow-employees whose business it will be to SERVE THE

PUBLIC EFFICIENTLY. In times past, employers, and employees have bartered among themselves, driving the best bargains they could with one another, not considering that in the final analysis they were, in reality, BARGAINING AT THE EXPENSE OF THE THIRD PARTY, THE PUBLIC THEY SERVED.

The depression served as a mighty protest from an injured public, whose rights had been trampled upon in every direction by those who were clamoring for individual advantages and profits. When the debris of the depression shall have been cleared away, and business shall have been once again restored to balance, both employers and employees will recognize that they are NO LONGER PRIVILEGED TO DRIVE BARGAINS AT THE EXPENSE OF THOSE WHOM THEY SERVE. The real employer of the future will be the public. This should be kept uppermost in mind by every person seeking to market personal services effectively.

Nearly every railroad in America is in financial difficulty. Who does not remember the day when, if a citizen enquired at the ticket office, the time of departure of a train, he was abruptly referred to the bulletin board instead of being politely given the information?

The street car companies have experienced a 'change of times' also. There was a time not so very long ago when street car conductors took pride in giving argument to passengers. Many of the street car tracks have been removed and passengers ride on a bus, whose driver is 'the last word in politeness.'

All over the country street car tracks are rusting from abandonment, or have been taken up. Whereever street cars are still in operation, passengers may now ride without argument, and one may even hail the car in the middle of the block, and the motorman will OBLIGINGLY pick him up.

HOW TIMES HAVE CHANGED! That is just the point I am trying to emphasize. TIMES HAVE CHANGED! Moreover, the change is reflected not merely in railroad offices and on street cars, but in other walks of life as well. The 'public-be-damned' policy is now passé. It has been supplanted by the 'we-are- obligingly-at-your-service, sir,' policy.

The bankers have learned a thing or two during this rapid change which has taken place during the past few years. Impoliteness on the part of a bank official, or bank employee today is as rare as it was conspicuous a dozen years ago. In the years past, some bankers (not all of them, of course), carried an atmosphere of austerity which gave every would-be borrower a chill when he even thought of approaching his banker for a loan.

The thousands of bank failures during the depression had the effect of removing the mahogany doors behind which bankers formerly barricaded themselves. They now sit at desks in the open, where they may be seen and approached at will by any depositor, or by anyone who wishes to see them, and the whole atmosphere of the bank is one of courtesy and understanding.

It used to be customary for customers to have to stand and wait at the corner grocery until the clerks were through passing the time of day with friends, and the proprietor had finished making up his bank deposit, before being waited upon. Chain stores, managed by COURTEOUS MEN who do everything in the way of service, short of shining the customer's shoes, have PUSHED THE OLD- TIME MERCHANTS INTO THE BACKGROUND. TIME MARCHES ON!

'Courtesy' and 'Service' are the watch-words of merchandising today, and apply to the person who is marketing personal services even more directly than to the employer whom he serves, because, in the final analysis, both the employer and his employee are EMPLOYED BY THE PUBLIC THEY SERVE. If they fail to serve well, they pay by the loss of their privilege of serving.

We can all remember the time when the gas-meter reader pounded on the door hard enough to break the panels. When the door was opened, he pushed his way in, uninvited, with a scowl on his face which plainly said, 'what-the-hell- did-you-keep-me-waiting- for?' All that has undergone a change. The meter-man now conducts himself as a gentleman who is 'delighted-to-be-at-your-service- sir.' Before the gas companies learned that their scowling meter-men were accumulating liabilities never to be cleared away, the polite salesmen of oil burners came along and did a land office business.

During the depression, I spent several months in the anthracite coal region of Pennsylvania, studying conditions which all but destroyed the coal industry. Among several very significant discoveries, was the fact that greed on the part of operators and their employees was the chief cause of the loss of business for the operators, and loss of jobs for the miners.

Through the pressure of a group of overzealous labor leaders, representing the employees, and the greed for profits on the part of the operators, the anthracite business suddenly dwindled. The coal operators and their employees drove sharp bargains with one another, adding the cost of the 'bargaining' to the price of the coal, until, finally, they discovered they had BUILT UP A WONDERFUL BUSINESS FOR THE MANUFACTURERS OF OIL BURNING OUTFITS AND THE PRODUCERS OF CRUDE OIL.

'The wages of sin is death!' Many have read this in the Bible, but few have discovered its meaning. Now, and for several years, the entire world has been listening BY FORCE, to a sermon which might well be called 'WHATSOEVER A MAN SOWETH, THAT SHALL HE ALSO REAP.'

Nothing as widespread and effective as the depression could possibly be 'just a coincidence.' Behind the depression was a CAUSE. Nothing ever happens without a CAUSE. In the main, the cause of the depression is traceable directly to the worldwide habit of trying to REAP without SOWING.

This should not be mistaken to mean that the depression represents a crop which the world is being FORCED to reap without having SOWN. The trouble is that the world *sowed the wrong sort of seed.* Any farmer knows he cannot sow the seed of thistles, and reap a harvest of grain. Beginning at the outbreak of the world war, the people of the world began to sow the seed of service inadequate in both quality and quantity. Nearly everyone was engaged in the pastime of trying to GET WITHOUT GIVING.

These illustrations are brought to the attention of those who have personal services to market, to show that we are where we are, and what we are, *because of our own conduct!* If there is a principle of cause and effect, which controls business, finance, and transportation, this same principle controls individuals and determines their economic status.

WHAT IS YOUR 'QQS' RATING?

The causes of success in marketing services EFFECTIVELY and permanently, have been clearly described. Unless those causes are studied, analyzed, understood and APPLIED, no man can market his services effectively and permanently. Every person must be his own salesman of personal services. The QUALITY and the QUANTITY of service rendered, and the SPIRIT in which it is rendered, determine to a large extent, the price, and the duration of employment. To market Personal services effectively, (which means a permanent market, at a satisfactory price, under pleasant conditions), one must adopt and follow the 'QQS' formula which means that QUALITY, plus QUANTITY, plus the proper SPIRIT of cooperation, equals perfect salesmanship of service. Remember the 'QQS' formula, but do more—APPLY IT AS A HABIT!

Let us analyze the formula to make sure we understand exactly what it means.

1. *QUALITY* of service shall be construed to mean the performance of every detail, in connection with your position, in the most efficient manner possible, with the object of greater efficiency always in mind.
2. *QUANTITY* of service shall be understood to mean the HABIT of rendering all the service of which you are capable, at all times, with the purpose of increasing the amount of service rendered as greater skill is developed through practice and experience. Emphasis is again placed on the word HABIT.
3. *SPIRIT* of service shall be construed to mean the HABIT of agreeable, armonious conduct which will induce cooperation from associates and fellow employees.

Adequacy of QUALITY and QUANTITY of service is not sufficient to maintain a permanent market for your services. The conduct, or the SPIRIT in which you deliver service, is a strong determining factor in connection with both the price you receive, and the duration of employment.

Andrew Carnegie stressed this point more than others in connection with his description of the factors which lead to success in the marketing of personal services. He emphasized again, and again, the necessity for HARMONIOUS CONDUCT. He stressed the fact that he would not retain any man, no matter how great a QUANTITY, or how efficient the QUALITY of his work, unless he worked in a spirit of HARMONY. Mr Carnegie insisted upon men being AGREEABLE.

To prove that he placed a high value upon this quality, he permitted many men *who conformed to his standards* to become very wealthy. Those who did not conform, had to make room for others.

The importance of a pleasing personality has been stressed, because it is a factor which enables one to render service in the proper SPIRIT. If one has a personality which PLEASES, and renders service in a spirit of HARMONY, these assets often make up for deficiencies in both the QUALITY, and the QUANTITY of service one renders. Nothing, however, can be SUCCESSFULLY SUBSTITUTED FOR PLEASING CONDUCT.

THE CAPITAL VALUE OF YOUR SERVICES

The person whose income is derived entirely from the sale of personal services is no less a merchant than the man who sells commodities, and it might well be added, such a person is subject to EXACTLY THE SAME RULES of conduct as the merchant who sells merchandise.

This has been emphasized, because the majority of people who live by the sale of personal services make the mistake of considering themselves free from the rules of conduct, and the responsibilities attached to those who are engaged in marketing commodities.

The new way of marketing services has practically forced both employer and employee into partnership alliances, through which both take into consideration the rights of the third party, THE PUBLIC THEY SERVE.

The day of the 'go-getter' has passed. He has been supplanted by the 'go- giver.' High-pressure methods in business finally blew the lid off. There will never be the need to put the lid back on, because, in the future, business will be conducted by methods that will require no pressure.

The actual capital value of your brains may be determined by the amount of income you can produce (by marketing your services). A fair estimate of the capital value of your services may be made by multiplying your annual income by sixteen and two-thirds, as it is reasonable to estimate that your annual income represents six percent of your capital value. Money rents for 6% per annum. Money is worth no more than brains. It is often worth much less.

Competent 'brains,' if effectively marketed, represent a much more desirable form of capital than that which is required to conduct a business dealing in commodities, because 'brains' are a form of capital which cannot be permanently depreciated through depressions, nor can this form of capital be stolen or spent. Moreover, the money which is essential for the conduct of business is as worthless as a sand dune, until it has been mixed with efficient 'brains.'

THE THIRTY MAJOR CAUSES OF FAILURE HOW MANY OF THESE ARE HOLDING YOU BACK?

Life's greatest tragedy consists of men and women who earnestly try, and fail! The tragedy lies in the overwhelmingly large majority of people who fail, as compared to the few who succeed.

I have had the privilege of analyzing several thousand men and women, 98% of whom were classed as 'failures.' There is something radically wrong with a civilization, and a system of education, which permit 98% of the people to go through life as failures. But I did not write this book for the purpose of moralizing on the rights and wrongs of the world; that would require a book a hundred times the size of this one.

My analysis work proved that there are thirty major reasons for failure, and thirteen major principles through which people accumulate fortunes. In this chapter, a description of the thirty major causes of failure will be given. As you go over the list, check yourself by it, point by point, for the purpose of discovering how many of these causes-of-failure stand between you and success.

1. UNFAVORABLE HEREDITARY BACKGROUND. There is but little, if anything, which can be done for people who are born with a deficiency in brain power. This philosophy offers but one method of bridging this weakness—through

the aid of the Master Mind. Observe with profit, however, that this is the ONLY one of the thirty causes of failure which may not be *easily corrected* by any individual.

2. LACK OF A WELL-DEFINED PURPOSE IN LIFE. There is no hope of success for the person who does not have a central purpose, or *definite goal* at which to aim. Ninety-eight out of every hundred of those whom I have analyzed, had no such aim. Perhaps this was the
3. LACK OF AMBITION TO AIM ABOVE MEDIOCRITY. We offer no hope for the person who is so indifferent as not to want to get ahead in life, and who is not willing to pay the price.
4. INSUFFICIENT EDUCATION. This is a handicap which may be overcome with comparative ease. Experience has proven that the best-educated people are often those who are known as 'self-made,' or self-educated. It takes more than a college degree to make one a person of education. Any person who is educated is one who has learned to get whatever he wants in life without violating the rights of others. Education consists, not so much of knowledge, but of knowledge effectively and persistently APPLIED. Men are paid, not merely for what they know, but more particularly for WHAT THEY DO WITH THAT WHICH THEY KNOW.
5. LACK OF SELF-DISCIPLINE. Discipline comes through self-control. This means that one must control all negative qualities. Before you can control conditions, you must first control yourself. Self-mastery is the hardest job you will ever tackle. If you do not conquer self, you will be conquered by self. You may see at one and the same time both your

best friend and your greatest enemy, by stepping in front of a mirror.

6. ILL HEALTH. No person may enjoy outstanding success without good health. Many of the causes of ill health are subject to mastery and control. These, in the main are:
   a. Overeating of foods not conducive to health
   b. Wrong habits of thought; giving expression to negatives.
   c. Wrong use of, and over indulgence in sex.
   d. Lack of proper physical exercise
   e. An inadequate supply of fresh air, due to improper breathing.
7. UNFAVORABLE ENVIRONMENTAL INFLUENCES DURING CHILDHOOD. 'As the twig is bent, so shall the tree grow.' Most people who have criminal tendencies acquire them as the result of bad environment, and improper associates during childhood.
8. PROCRASTINATION. This is one of the most common causes of failure. 'Old Man Procrastination' stands within the shadow of every human being, waiting his opportunity to spoil one's chances of success. Most of us go through life as failures, because we are waiting for the 'time to be right' to start doing something worthwhile. Do not wait. The time will never be 'just right.' Start where you stand, and work with whatever tools you may have at your command, and better tools will be found as you go along.
9. LACK OF PERSISTENCE. Most of us are good 'starters' but poor 'finishers' of everything we begin. Moreover, people are prone to give up at the first signs of defeat. There is no substitute for PERSISTENCE. The person who makes PERSISTENCE his watch-word, discovers that 'Old Man

Failure' finally becomes tired, and makes his departure. Failure cannot cope with PERSISTENCE.

10. NEGATIVE PERSONALITY. There is no hope of success for the person who repels people through a negative personality. Success comes through the application of POWER, and power is attained through the cooperative efforts of other people. A negative personality will not induce cooperation.
11. LACK OF CONTROLLED SEXUAL URGE. Sex energy is the most powerful of all the stimuli which move people into ACTION. Because it is the most powerful of the emotions, it must be controlled, through transmutation, and converted into other channels.
12. UNCONTROLLED DESIRE FOR 'SOMETHING FOR NOTHING.' The gambling instinct drives millions of people to failure. Evidence of this may be found in a study of the Wall Street crash of '29, during which millions of people tried to make money by gambling on stock margins.
13. LACK OF A WELL DEFINED POWER OF DECISION. Men who succeed reach decisions promptly, and change them, if at all, very slowly. Men who fail, reach decisions, if at all, very slowly, and change them frequently, and quickly. Indecision and procrastination are twin brothers. Where one is found, the other may usually be found also. Kill off this pair before they completely 'hog-tie' you to the treadmill of FAILURE.
14. ONE OR MORE OF THE SIX BASIC FEARS. These fears have been analyzed for you in a later chapter. They must be mastered before you can market your services effectively.

15. WRONG SELECTION OF A MATE IN MARRIAGE. This a most common cause of failure. The relationship of marriage brings people intimately into contact. Unless this relationship is harmonious, failure is likely to follow. Moreover, it will be a form of failure that is marked by misery and unhappiness, destroying all signs of AMBITION.
16. OVER-CAUTION. The person who takes no chances, generally has to take whatever is left when others are through choosing. Over-caution is as bad as under-caution. Both are extremes to be guarded against. Life itself is filled with the element of chance.
17. WRONG SELECTION OF ASSOCIATES IN BUSINESS. This is one of the most common causes of failure in business. In marketing personal services, one should use great care to select an employer who will be an inspiration, and who is, himself, intelligent and successful. We emulate those with whom we associate most closely. Pick an employer who is worth emulating.
18. SUPERSTITION AND PREJUDICE. Superstition is a form of fear. It is also a sign of ignorance. Men who succeed keep open minds and are afraid of nothing.
19. WRONG SELECTION OF A VOCATION. No man can succeed in a line of endeavor which he does not like. The most essential step in the marketing of personal services is that of selecting an occupation into which you can throw yourself wholeheartedly.
20. LACK OF CONCENTRATION OF EFFORT. The 'jack-of- all-trades' seldom is good at any. Concentrate all of your efforts on one DEFINITE CHIEF AIM.
21. THE HABIT OF INDISCRIMINATE SPENDING.

The spend-thrift cannot succeed, mainly because he stands eternally in FEAR OF POVERTY. Form the habit of systematic saving by putting aside a definite percentage of your income. Money in the bank gives one a very safe foundation of COURAGE when bargaining for the sale of personal services. Without money, one must take what one is offered, and be glad to get it.

22. LACK OF ENTHUSIASM. Without enthusiasm one cannot be convincing. Moreover, enthusiasm is contagious, and the person who has it, under control, is generally welcome in any group of people.
23. INTOLERANCE. The person with a 'closed' mmd on any subject seldom gets ahead. Intolerance means that one has stopped acquiring knowledge. The most damaging forms of intolerance are those connected with religious, racial, and political differences of opinion.
24. INTEMPERANCE. The most damaging forms of intemperance are connected with eating, strong drink, and sexual activities. Overindulgence in any of these is fatal to success.
25. INABILITY TO COOPERATE WITH OTHERS. More people lose their positions and their big opportunities in life, because of this fault, than for all other reasons combined. It is a fault which no well-informed business man, or leader will tolerate.
26. POSSESSION OF POWER THAT WAS NOT ACQUIRED THROUGH SELF EFFORT. (Sons and daughters of wealthy men, and others who inherit money which they did not earn). Power in the hands of one who did not acquire it gradually, is often fatal to success.

QUICK RICHES are more dangerous than poverty.

27. INTENTIONAL DISHONESTY. There is no substitute for honesty. One may be temporarily dishonest by force of circumstances over which one has no control, without permanent damage. But, there is NO HOPE for the person who is dishonest by choice. Sooner or later, his deeds will catch up with him, and he will pay by loss of reputation, and perhaps even loss of liberty.
28. EGOTISM AND VANITY. These qualities serve as red lights which warn others to keep away. THEY ARE FATAL TO SUCCESS.
29. GUESSING INSTEAD OF THINKING. Most people are too indifferent or lazy to acquire FACTS with which to THINK ACCURATELY. They prefer to act on 'opinions' created by guesswork or snap-judgments.
30. LACK OF CAPITAL. This is a common cause of failure among those who start out in business for the first time, without sufficient reserve of capital to absorb the shock of their mistakes, and to carry them over until they have established a REPUTATION.
31. Under this, name any particular cause of failure from which you have suffered that has not been included in the foregoing list.

In these thirty major causes of failure is found a description of the tragedy of life, which obtains for practically every person who tries and fails. It will be helpful if you can induce someone who knows you well to go over this list with you, and help to analyze you by the thirty causes of failure. It may be beneficial if you try this alone. Most people cannot see themselves as others see them. You may be one who cannot.

The oldest of admonitions is 'Man, know thyself!' If you market merchandise successfully, you must know the merchandise. The same is true in marketing personal services. You should know all of your weaknesses in order that you may either bridge them or eliminate them entirely. You should know your strength in order that you may call attention to it when selling your services. You can know yourself only through *accurate* analysis.

The folly of ignorance in connection with self was displayed by a young man who applied to the manager of a well known business for a position. He made a very good impression until the manager asked him what salary he expected. He replied that he had no fixed sum in mind (*lack of a definite aim*). The manager then said, 'We will pay you all you are worth, alter we try you out for a week.'

'I will not accept it,' the applicant replied, 'because I AM GETTING MORE THAN THAT WHERE I AM NOW EMPLOYED.'

Before you even start to negotiate for a readjustment of your salary in your present position, or to seek employment elsewhere, BE SURE THAT YOU ARE WORTH MORE THAN YOU NOW RECEIVE.

It is one thing to WANT money—everyone wants more—but it is something entirely different to be WORTH MORE! Many people mistake their WANTS for their JUST DUES. Your financial requirements or wants have nothing whatever to do with your WORTH. Your value is established entirely by your ability to render useful service or your capacity to induce others to render such service.

TAKE INVENTORY OF YOURSELF: 28 QUESTIONS YOU SHOULD ANSWER

Annual self-analysis is an essential in the effective marketing of personal services, as is annual inventory in merchandising. Moreover, the yearly analysis should disclose a DECREASE IN FAULTS, and an increase in VIRTUES. One goes ahead, stands still, or goes backward in life. One's object should be, of course, to go ahead. Annual self-analysis will disclose whether advancement has been, made, and if so, how much. It will also disclose any backward steps one may have made. The effective marketing of personal services requires one to move forward even if the progress is slow.

Your annual self-analysis should be made at the end of each year, so you can include in your New Year's Resolutions any improvements which the analysis indicates should be made. Take this inventory by asking yourself the following questions, and by checking your answers with the aid of someone who will not permit you to deceive yourself as to their accuracy.

SELF-ANALYSIS QUESTIONNAIRE FOR PERSONAL INVENTORY

1. Have I attained the goal which I established as my objective for this year? (You should work with a definite yearly objective to be attained as a part of your major life objective).
2. Have I delivered service of the best possible QUALITY of which I was capable, or could I have improved any part of this service?
3. Have I delivered service in the greatest possible QUANTITY

of which I was capable?

4. Has the spirit of my conduct been harmonious, and cooperative at all times?
5. Have I permitted the habit of PROCRSTINATION to decrease my efficiency, and if so, to what extent?
6. Have I improved my PERSONALITY, and if so, in what ways?
7. Have I been PERSISTENT in following my plans through to completion?
8. Have I reached DECISIONS PROMPTLY AND DEFINITELY on all occasions?
9. Have I permitted any one or more of the six basic fears to decrease my efficiency?
10. Have I been either 'over-cautious,' or 'under-cautious?"
11. Has my relationship with my associates in work been pleasant, or unpleasant? If it has been unpleasant, has the fault been partly, or wholly mine?
12. Have I dissipated any of my energy through lack of CONCENTRATION of effort?
13. Have I been open minded and tolerant in connection with all subjects?
14. In what way have I improved my ability to render service?
15. Have I been intemperate in any of my habits?
16. Have I expressed, either openly or secretly, any form of EGOTISM?
17. Has my conduct toward my associates been such that it has induced them to RESPECT me?
18. Have my opinions and DECISIONS been based upon guesswork, or accuracy of analysis and THOUGHT?

19. Have I followed the habit of budgeting my time, my expenses, and my income, and have I been conservative in these budgets?
20. How much time have I devoted to UNPROFITABLE effort which I might have used to better advantage?
21. How may I RE-BUDGET my time, and change my habits so I will be more efficient during the coming year?
22. Have I been guilty of any conduct which was not approved by my conscience?
23. In what ways have I rendered MORE SERVICE AND BETTER SERVICE than I was paid to render?
24. Have I been unfair to anyone, and if so, in what way?
25. If I had been the purchaser of my own services for the year, would I be satisfied with my purchase?
26. Am I in the right vocation, and if not, why not?
27. Has the purchaser of my services been satisfied with the service I have rendered, and if not, why not?
28. What is my present rating on the fundamental principles of success? (Make this rating fairly, and frankly, and have it checked by someone who is courageous enough to do it accurately).

Having read and assimilated the information conveyed through this chapter, you are now ready to create a practical plan for marketing your personal services. In this chapter will be found an adequate description of every principle essential in planning the sale of personal services, including the major attributes of leadership; the most common causes of failure in leadership; a description of the fields of opportunity for leadership; the main causes of failure in all walks of life, and the important questions which should be used in self-analysis. This extensive and detailed presentation of accurate information has been included, because it will be needed *by* all who must begin the accumulation of riches by marketing personal services. Those who have lost their fortunes, and those who are just beginning to earn money, have nothing but personal services to offer in return for riches, therefore it is essential that they have available the practical information needed to market services to best advantage.

The information contained in this chapter will be of great value to all who aspire to attain leadership in any calling. It will be particularly helpful to those aiming to market their services as business or industrial executives.

Complete assimilation and understanding of the information here conveyed will be helpful in marketing one's own services, and it will also help one to become more analytical and capable of judging people. The information will be priceless to personnel directors, employment managers, and other executives charged with the selection of employees, and the maintenance of efficient organizations. If you doubt this statement, test its soundness by answering in writing the twenty-eight self-analysis questions. That might be both interesting and profitable, even though you do not doubt the soundness of the statement.

WHERE AND HOW ONE MAY FIND OPPORTUNITIES TO ACCUMULATE RICHES

Now that we have analyzed the principles by which riches may be accumulated, we naturally ask, 'where may one find favorable opportunities to apply these principles?' Very well, let us take inventory and see what the United States of America offer the person seeking riches, great or small.

To begin with, let us remember, all of us, that we live in a country where every law-abiding citizen enjoys freedom of thought and freedom of deed unequaled *anywhere in the world.* Most of us have never taken inventory of the advantages of this freedom. We have never compared our unlimited freedom with the curtailed freedom in other countries.

Here we have freedom of thought, freedom in the choice and enjoyment of education, freedom in religion, freedom in politics, freedom in the choice of a business, profession or occupation, freedom to accumulate and own without molestation, *ALL THE PROPERTY WE CAN ACCUMULATE,* freedom to choose our place of residence, freedom in marriage, freedom through equal opportunity to all races, freedom of travel from one state to another, freedom in our choice of foods, and freedom to *AIM FOR ANY STATION IN LIFE FOR WHICH WE HAVE PREPARED OURSELVES,* even for the presidency of the United States.

We have other forms of freedom, but this list will give a bird's eye view of the most important, which constitute OPPORTUNITY of the highest order. This advantage of freedom is all the more conspicuous because the United States is the only country guaranteeing to every citizen, whether native born or naturalized, so broad and varied a list of freedom.

Next, let us recount some of the blessings which our widespread freedom has placed within our hands. Take the average American family for example (meaning, the family of average income) and sum up the benefits available to every member of the family, in this land of OPPORTUNITY and plenty!

a. FOOD. Next to freedom of thought and deed comes FOOD, CLOTHING, and SHELTER, the three basic necessities of life.

Because of our universal freedom the average American family has available, at its very door, the choicest selection of food to be found anywhere in the world, and at prices within its financial range.

A family of two, living in the heart of Times Square district of New York City, far removed from the source of production of foods, took careful inventory of the cost of a simple breakfast, with this astonishing result:

Articles of food;	*Cost at the breakfast table:*
Grape Fruit Juice (From Florida)…	02
Rippled Wheat Breakfast food (Kansas Farm)…	02
Tea (From China)…	02
Bananas (From South America)…	02½
Toasted Bread (From Kansas Farm)…	01
Fresh Country Eggs (From Utah)…	07
Sugar (From Cuba, or Utah)…	00½
Butter and Cream (From New England)…	03
Grand total…	20

It is not very difficult to obtain FOOD in a country where two people can have breakfast consisting of all they want or need for a dime apiece! Observe that this simple breakfast was gathered, by some strange form of magic (?) from China, South America,

Utah, Kansas and the New England States, and delivered on the breakfast table, ready for consumption, in the very heart of the most crowded city in America, at a cost well within the means of the most humble laborer.

The cost included all federal, state and city taxes! (Here is a fact the politicians did not mention when they were crying out to the voters to throw their opponents out of office because the people were being taxed to death).

b. SHELTER. This family lives in a comfortable apartment, heated by steam, lighted with electricity, with gas for cooking, all for $65.00 a month. In a smaller city, or a more sparsely settled part of New York city, the same apartment could be had for as low as $20.00 a month.

The toast they had for breakfast in the food estimate was toasted on an electric toaster, which cost but a few dollars, the apartment is cleaned with a vacuum sweeper that is run by electricity. Hot &nd cold water is available, at all times, in the kitchen and the bathroom. The food is kept cool in a refrigerator that is run by electricity. The wife curls her hair, washes her clothes and irons them with easily operated electrical equipment, on power obtained by sticking a plug in the wall. The husband shaves with an electric shaver, and they receive entertainment from all over the world, twenty four hours a day, if they want it, without cost, by merely turning the dial of their radio.

There are other conveniences in this apartment, but the foregoing list will give a fair idea of some of the concrete evidences of the freedom we, of America, enjoy. (And this is neither political nor economic propaganda).

c. CLOTHING. Anywhere in the United States, the woman

of average clothing requirements can dress very comfortably and neatly for less than $200.00 a year, and the average man can dress for the same, or less.

Only the three basic necessities of food, clothing, and shelter have been mentioned. The average American citizen has other privileges and advantages available in return for modest effort, not exceeding eight hours per day of labor. Among these is the privilege of automobile transportation, with which one can go and come at will, at very small cost.

The average American has security of property rights not found in any other country in the world. He can place his surplus money in a bank with the assurance that his government will protect it, and make good to him if the bank fails. If an American citizen wants to travel from one state to another he needs no passport, no one's permission. He may go when he pleases, and return at will. Moreover, he may travel by train, private automobile, bus, airplane, or ship, as his pocketbook permits. In Germany, Russia, Italy, and most of the other European and Oriental countries, the people cannot travel with so much freedom, and at so little cost.

THE 'MIRACLE' THAT HAS PROVIDED THESE BLESSINGS

We often hear politicians proclaiming the freedom of America, when they solicit votes, but seldom do they take the time or devote sufficient effort to the analysis of the source or nature of this 'freedom.' Having no axe to grind, no grudge to express, no ulterior motives to be carried out, I have the privilege of going into a frank analysis of that mysterious, abstract, greatly misunderstood 'SOMETHING' which gives to every citizen of America more blessings, more opportunities to accumulate wealth, more freedom of every nature, than may be found in any other country.

I have the right to analyze the source and nature of this UNSEEN POWER, because I know, and have known for more than a quarter of a century, many of the men who organized that power, and many who are now responsible for its maintenance.

The name of this mysterious benefactor of mankind is CAPITAL!

CAPITAL consists not alone of money, but more particularly of highly organized, intelligent groups of men who plan ways and means of using money efficiently for the good of the public, and profitably to themselves.

These groups consist of scientists, educators, chemists, inventors, business analysts, publicity men, transportation experts, accountants, lawyers, doctors, and both men and women who have highly specialized knowledge in all fields of industry and business. They pioneer, experiment, and blaze trails in new fields of endeavor. They support colleges, hospitals, public schools, build good roads, publish newspapers, pay most of the cost of government, and take care of the multitudinous detail essential to human progress. Stated briefly, the capitalists are the brains of civilization, because they supply the entire fabric of which all education, enlightenment and human progress consists.

Money, without brains, always is dangerous. Properly used, it is the most important essential of civilization. The simple breakfast here described could not have been delivered to the New York family at a dime each, *or at any other price*, if organized capital had not provided the machinery, the ships, the railroads, and the huge armies of trained men to operate them.

Some slight idea of the importance of ORGANIZED CAPITAL may be had by trying to imagine yourself burdened with the responsibility of collecting, without the aid of capital, and delivering to the New York City family, the simple breakfast described.

To supply the tea, you would have to make a trip to China or India, both a very long way from America. Unless you are an excellent swimmer, you would become rather tired before making the round trip. Then, too, another problem would confront you. What would you use for money, even if you had the physical endurance to swim the ocean?

To supply the sugar, you would have to take another long swim to Cuba, or a long walk to the sugar beet section of Utah. But even then, you might come back without the sugar, because organized effort and money are necessary to produce sugar, to say nothing of what is required to refine, transport, and deliver it to the breakfast table anywhere in the United States.

The eggs, you could deliver easily enough from the barn yards near New York City, but you would have a very long walk to Florida and return, before you could serve the two glasses of grapefruit juice.

You would have another long walk, to Kansas, or one of the other wheat growing states, when you went after the four slices of wheat bread.

The Rippled Wheat Biscuits would have to be omitted from the menu, because they would not be available except through the labor of a trained organization of men and suitable machinery, ALL OF WHICH CALL FOR CAPITAL.

While resting, you could take off for another little swim

down to South

America, where you would pick up a couple of bananas, and on your return, you could take a short walk to the nearest farm having a dairy and pick up some butter and cream. Then your New York City family would be ready to sit down and enjoy breakfast, and *you could collect your two dimes for your labor!*

Seems absurd, doesn't it? Well, the procedure described would be the only possible way these simple items of food could be delivered to the heart of New York City, if we had no capitalistic system.

The sum of money required for the building and maintenance of the railroads and steam ships used in the delivery of that simple breakfast is so huge that it staggers one's imagination. It runs into hundreds of millions of dollars, not to mention the armies of trained employees required to man the ships and trains. But, transportation is only a part of the requirements of modern civilization in capitalistic America. Before there can be anything to haul, something must be grown from the ground, or manufactured and prepared for market. This calls for more millions of dollars for equipment, machinery, boxing, marketing, and for the wages of millions of men and women.

Steam ships and railroads do not spring up from the earth and function automatically. They come in response to the call of civilization, through the labor and ingenuity and organizing ability of men who have IMAGINATION, FAITH,

ENTHUSIASM, DECISION, PERSISTENCE! These men are known as capitalists. They are motivated by the desire to build, construct, achieve, render useful service, earn profits and accumulate riches. And, because they RENDER SERVICE WITHOUT WHICH THERE WOULD BE NO

CIVILIZATION, they put themselves in the way of great riches.

Just to keep the record simple and understandable, I will add that these capitalists are the self-same men of whom most of us have heard soap-box orators speak. They are the same men to whom radicals, racketeers, dishonest politicians and grafting labor leaders refer as 'the predatory interests,' or 'Wall Street.'

I am not attempting to present a brief for or against any group of men or any system of economics. I am not attempting to condemn collective bargaining when I refer to 'grafting labor leaders,' nor do I aim to give a clean bill of health to all individuals known as capitalists.

The purpose of this book—*A purpose to which I have faithfully devoted over a quarter of a century*—is to present to all who want the knowledge, the most dependable philosophy through which individuals may accumulate riches in whatever amounts they desire.

I have here analyzed the economic advantages of the capitalistic system for the two-fold purpose of showing:

1. that all who seek riches must recognize and adapt themselves to the system that controls all approaches to fortunes, large or small, and
2. to present the side of the picture opposite to that being shown by politicians and demagogues who deliberately becloud the issues they bring up, by referring to organized capital as if it were something poisonous.

This is a capitalistic country, it was developed through the use of capital, and we who claim the right to partake of the blessings of freedom and opportunity, we who seek to accumulate riches here, may as well know that neither riches nor opportunity would be available to us if ORGANIZED CAPITAL had not provided these benefits.

For more than twenty years it has been a somewhat popular and growing pastime for radicals, self-seeking politicians, racketeers, crooked labor leaders, and on occasion religious leaders, to take pot-shots at 'WALL STREET, THE MONEY CHANGERS, and BIG BUSINESS.'

The practice became so general that we witnessed during the business depression, the unbelievable sight of high government officials lining up with the cheap politicians, and labor leaders, with the openly avowed purpose of throttling the system which has made Industrial America the richest country on earth. The line-up was so general and so well organized that it prolonged the worst depression America has ever known. It cost millions of men their jobs, because those jobs were inseparably a part of the industrial and capitalistic system which form the very backbone of the nation.

During this unusual alliance of government officials and self-seeking individuals who were endeavoring to profit by declaring 'open season' on the American system of industry, a certain type of labor leader joined forces with the politicians and offered to deliver voters in return for legislation designed to permit men to TAKE RICHES AWAY FROM INDUSTRY BY ORGANIZED FORCE OF NUMBERS, INSTEAD OF THE BETTER METHOD OF GIVING A FAIR DAY's WORK FOR A FAIR DAY's PAY.

Millions of men and women throughout the nation are still engaged in this popular pastime of trying to GET without GIVING. Some of them are lined up with labor unions, where they demand SHORTER HOURS AND MORE PAY! Others do not take the trouble to work at all. THEY DEMAND GOVERNMENT RELIEF AND ARE GETTING IT. Their idea of their rights of freedom was demonstrated in New York City, where violent complaint was registered with the Postmaster, by a group of 'relief beneficiaries,' because the Postmen awakened them at 7: 30 A. M. to deliver Government relief checks. They DEMANDED that the time of delivery be set up to 10: 00 o'clock.

If you are one of those who believe that riches can be accumulated by the mere act of men who organize themselves into groups and demand MORE PAY for LESS SERVICE, if you are one of those who DEMAND Government relief without early morning disturbance when the money is delivered to you, if you are one of those who believe in trading their votes to politicians in return for the passing of laws which permit the raiding of the public treasury, you may rest securely on your belief, with certain knowledge that no one will disturb you, because THIS IS A FREE COUNTRY WHERE EVERY MAN MAY THINK AS HE PLEASES, where nearly everybody can live with but little effort, where many may live well without doing any work whatsoever.

However, you should know the full truth concerning this FREEDOM of which so many people boast, and so few understand. As great as it is, as far as it reaches, as many privileges as it provides, IT DOES NOT, AND CANNOT BRING RICHES WITHOUT EFFORT.

There is but one dependable method of accumulating, and legally holding riches, and that is by rendering useful service. No system has ever been created by which men can legally acquire riches through mere force of numbers, or without giving in return an equivalent value of one form or another.

There is a principle known as the law of ECONOMICS! This is more than a theory. It is a law no man can beat.

Mark well the name of the principle, and remember it, because it is far more powerful than all the politicians and political machines. It is above and beyond the control of all the labor unions. It cannot be swayed, nor influenced nor bribed by racketeers or self-appointed leaders in any calling. Moreover, IT HAS AN ALL-SEEING EYE, AND A PERFECT SYSTEM OF BOOKKEEPING, in which it keeps an accurate account of the transactions of every human being engaged in the business of trying to get without giving. Sooner or later its auditors come around, look over the records of individuals both great and small, and demand an accounting.

'Wall Street, Big Business, Capital Predatory Interests,' or whatever name you choose to give the system which has given us AMERICAN FREEDOM, represents a group of men who understand, respect, and adapt themselves to this powerful LAW OF ECONOMICS! Their financial continuation depends upon their respecting the law.

Most people living in America like this country, its capitalistic system and all. I must confess I know of no better country, where one may find greater opportunities to accumulate riches. Judging by their acts and deeds, there are some in this country who do not like it. That, of course is their privilege; if they do not like this country, its capitalistic system, its boundless opportunities, *THEY HAVE THE PRIVILEGE OF CLEARING OUT!* Always there are other countries, such as Germany, Russia, and Italy, where one may try one's hand at enjoying freedom, and accumulating riches providing one is not too particular.

America provides all the freedom and all the opportunity to accumulate riches that any honest person may require. When one goes hunting for game, one selects hunting grounds where game is plentiful. When seeking riches, the same rule would naturally obtain.

If it is riches you are seeking, do not overlook the possibilities of a country whose citizens are so rich that women, alone, spend over two hundred million dollars annually for lip-sticks, rouge and cosmetics. Think twice, you who are seeking riches, before trying to destroy the Capitalistic System of a country whose citizens spend over fifty million dollars a year for GREETING CARDS, with which to express their appreciation of their FREEDOM!

If it is money you are seeking, consider carefully a country that spends hundreds of millions of dollars annually for cigarettes, the bulk of the income from which goes to only four major companies engaged in supplying this national builder of 'non-chalance' and 'quiet nerves.'

By all means give plenty of consideration to a country whose people spend annually more than fifteen million dollars for the privilege of seeing moving pictures, and toss in a few additional mil-lions for liquor, narcotics, and other less potent soft drinks and giggle-waters.

Do not be in too big a hurry to get away from a country whose people willingly, even eagerly, hand over millions of dollars annually for football, baseball, and prize fights.

And, by all means, STICK by a country whose inhabitants give up more than a million dollars a year for chewing gum, and another million for safety razor blades.

Remember, also, that this is but the beginning of the

available sources for the accumulation of wealth. Only a few of the luxuries and non-essentials have been mentioned. But, remember that the business of producing, transporting, and marketing these few items of merchandise gives regular employment to MANY MILLIONS OF MEN AND WOMEN, who receive for their services MANY MILLIONS OF DOLLARS MONTHLY, and spend it freely for both the luxuries and the necessities.

Especially remember, that back of all this exchange of merchandise and personal services may be found an abundance of OPPORTUNITY to accumulate riches. Here our AMERICAN FREE-DOM comes to one's aid. There is nothing to stop you, or anyone from engaging in any portion of the effort necessary to carry on these businesses. If one has superior talent, training, experience, one may accumulate riches in large amounts. Those not so fortunate may accumulate smaller amounts. Anyone may earn a living in return for a very nominal amount of labor.

So—there you are!

OPPORTUNITY has spread its wares before you. Step up to the front, select what you want, create your plan, put the plan into action, and follow through with PERSISTENCE. 'Capitalistic' America will do the rest. You can depend upon this much—CAPITALISTIC AMERICA INSURES EVERY PERSON THE OPPORTUNITY TO RENDER USEFUL SERVICE, AND TO COLLECT RICHES IN PROPORTION TO THE VALUE OF THE SERVICE.

The 'System' denies no one this right, but it does not, and cannot promise SOMETHING FOR NOTHING, because the system, itself, is irrevocably controlled by the LAW OF ECONOMICS which neither recognizes nor tolerates for long,

GETTING WITHOUT GIVING.

The LAW OF ECONOMICS was passed by Nature! There is no Supreme Court to which violators of this law may appeal. The law hands out both penalties for its violation, and appropriate rewards for its observance, without interference or the possibility of interference by any human being. The law cannot be repealed. It is as fixed as the stars in the heavens, and subject to, and a part of the same system that controls the stars.

May one refuse to adapt one's self to the LAW OF ECONOMICS?

Certainly! This is a free country, where all men are born with equal rights, including the privilege of ignoring the LAW OF ECONOMICS.

What happens then?

Well, nothing happens until large numbers of men join forces for the avowed purpose of ignoring the law, and taking what they want by force.

THEN COMES THE DICTATOR, WITH WELL ORGANIZED FIRING SQUADS AND MACHINE GUNS!

We have not yet reached that stage in America! But we have heard all we want to know about how the system works. Perhaps we hall be fortunate enough not to demand personal knowledge of so gruesome a reality. Doubtless we shall prefer to continue with our FREEDOM OF SPEECH, FREEDOM OF DEED, and FREEDOM TO RENDER USEFUL SERVICE IN RETURN FOR RICHES.

The practice, by Government officials of extending to men and women the privilege of raiding the public treasury in return for votes, sometimes results in election, but as night follows day, the final payoff comes; when every penny wrongfully used, must be repaid with compound interest on compound interest. If those who make the grab are not forced to repay, the burden falls on their children, and their children's children, 'even unto the third and fourth generations.' There is no way to avoid the debt.

Men can, and sometimes do, form themselves into groups for the purpose of crowding wages up, and working hours down. There is a point beyond which they cannot go. It is the point at which the LAW OF ECONOMICS steps in, and the sheriff gets both the employer and the employees.

For six years, from 1929, to 1935, the people of America, both rich and poor, barely missed seeing the Old Man Economics hand over to the sheriff all the businesses, and industries and banks. It was not a pretty sight! It did not increase our respect for mob psychology through which men cast reason to the winds and start trying to GET without GIVING.

We who went through those six discouraging years, when FEAR WAS IN THE SADDLE, AND FAITH WAS ON THE GROUND, cannot forget how ruthlessly the LAW OF ECONOMICS exacted its toll from both rich and poor, weak and strong, old and young. We shall not wish to go through another such experience.

These observations are not founded upon short-time experience. They are the result of twenty-five years of careful analysis of the methods of both the most successful and the most unsuccessful men America has known.

3

POWER OF THE MASTER MIND
The Driving Force

THE NINTH STEP TOWARD RICHES

Power is essential for success in the accumulation of money.

PLANS are inert and useless, without sufficient POWER to translate them into ACTION. This chapter will describe the method by which an individual may attain and apply POWER.

POWER may be defined as 'organized and intelligently directed KNOWLEDGE.' Power, as the term is here used, refers to ORGANIZED effort, sufficient to enable an individual to transmute DESIRE into its monetary equivalent. ORGANIZED effort is produced through the coordination of effort of two or more people, who work toward a DEFINITE end, in a spirit of harmony.

POWER IS REQUIRED FOR THE ACCUMULATION OF MONEY! POWER IS NECESSARY FOR THE RETENTION OF MONEY AFTER IT HAS BEEN ACCUMULATED!

Let us ascertain how power may be acquired. If power is 'organized knowledge,' let us examine the sources of knowledge:

a. INFINITE INTELLIGENCE. This source of knowledge may be contacted through the procedure described in another chapter, with the aid of Creative Imagination.
b. ACCUMULATED EXPERIENCE. The accumulated experience of man, (or that portion of it which has been organized and recorded), may be found in any well-equipped public library. An important part of this accumulated experience is taught in public schools and colleges, where it has been classified and organized.
c. EXPERIMENT AND RESEARCH. In the field of science, and in practically every other walk of life, men are gathering, classifying, and organizing new facts daily. This is the source to which one must turn when knowledge is not available through 'accumulated experience.' Here, too, the Creative Imagination must often be used.

Knowledge may be acquired from any of the foregoing sources. It may be converted into POWER by organizing it into definite PLANS and by expressing those plans in terms of ACTION.

Examination of the three major sources of knowledge will readily disclose the difficulty an individual would have, if he depended upon his efforts alone, in assembling knowledge and expressing it through definite plans in terms of ACTION. If his plans are comprehensive, and if they contemplate large proportions, he must, generally, induce others to cooperate with him, before he can inject into them the necessary element of POWER.

GAINING POWER THROUGH THE 'MASTER MIND'

The 'Master Mind' may be defined as: 'Coordination of knowledge and effort, in a spirit of harmony, between two or more people, for the attainment of a definite purpose.'

No individual may have great power without availing himself of the 'Master Mind.' In a preceding chapter, instructions were given for the creation of PLANS for the purpose of translating DESIRE into its monetary equivalent. If you carry out these instructions with PERSISTENCE and intelligence, and use discrimination in the selection of your 'Master Mind' group, your objective will have been half-way reached, even before you begin to recognize it.

So you may better understand the 'intangible' potentialities of power available to you, through a properly chosen 'Master Mind' group, we will here explain the two characteristics of the Master Mind principle, one of which is economic in nature, and the other psychic. The economic feature is obvious. Economic advantages may be created by any person who surrounds himself with the advice, counsel, and personal cooperation of a group of men who are willing to lend him wholehearted aid, in a spirit of PERFECT HARMONY. This form of cooperative alliance has been the basis of nearly every great fortune. Your understanding of this great truth may definitely determine your financial status.

The psychic phase of the Master Mind principle is much more abstract, much more difficult to comprehend, because it has reference to the spiritual forces with which the human race, as a whole, is not well acquainted. You may catch a significant suggestion from this statement: 'No two minds ever come together without, thereby, creating a third, invisible, intangible force which may be likened to a third mind.'

Keep in mind the fact that there are only two known elements in the whole universe, energy and matter. It is a well known fact that matter may be broken down into units of molecules, atoms, and electrons. There are units of matter which may be isolated, separated, and analyzed.

Likewise, there are units of energy.

The human mind is a form of energy, a part of it being spiritual in nature. When the minds of two people are coordinated in a SPIRIT OF HARMONY, the spiritual units of energy of each mind form an affinity, which constitutes the 'psychic' phase of the Master Mind.

The Master Mind principle, or rather the economic feature of it, was first called to my attention by Andrew Carnegie, over twenty-five years ago. Discovery of this principle was responsible for the choice of my life's work.

Mr Carnegie's Master Mind group consisted of a staff of approximately fifty men, with whom he surrounded himself, for the DEFINITE PURPOSE of manufacturing and marketing steel. He attributed his entire fortune to the POWER he accumulated through this 'Master Mind.'

Analyze the record of any man who has accumulated a great fortune, and many of those who have accumulated modest fortunes, and you will find that they have either consciously, or unconsciously employed the 'Master Mind' principle.

GREAT POWER CAN BE ACCUMULATED THROUGH NO OTHER PRINCIPLE!

ENERGY is Nature's universal set of building blocks, out of which she constructs every material thing in the universe, including man, and every form of animal and vegetable life.

Through a process which only Nature completely understands, she translates energy into matter.

Nature's building blocks are available to man, in the energy involved in THINKING! Man's brain may be compared to an electric battery. It absorbs energy from the ether, which permeates every atom of matter, and fills the entire universe.

It is a well known fact that a group of electric batteries will provide more energy than a single battery. It is also a well known fact that an individual battery will provide energy in proportion to the number and capacity of the cells it contains.

The brain functions in a similar fashion. This accounts for the fact that some brains are more efficient than others, and leads to this significant statement—a group of brains coordinated (or connected) in a spirit of harmony, will provide more thought-energy than a single brain, just as a group of electric batteries will provide more energy than a single battery.

Through this metaphor it becomes immediately obvious that the Master Mind principle holds the secret of the POWER wielded by men who surround themselves with other men of brains.

There follows, now, another statement which will lead still nearer to an understanding of the psychic phase of the Master Mind principle: When a group of individual brains are coordinated and function in Harmony, the increased energy created through that alliance, becomes available to every individual brain in the group.

It is a well known fact that Henry Ford began his business career under the handicap of poverty, illiteracy, and ignorance. It is an equally well known fact that, within the inconceivably short period of ten years, Mr Ford mastered these three handicaps, and that within twenty-five years he made himself one of the richest men in America. Connect with this fact, the additional knowledge that Mr Ford's most rapid strides became noticeable, from the time he became a personal friend of Thomas A. Edison, and you will begin to understand what the influence of one mind upon another can accomplish. Go a step farther, and consider the fact that Mr Ford's most outstanding achievements began from the time that he formed the acquaintances of Harvey Firestone, John Burroughs, and Luther Burbank, (each a man of great brain capacity), and you will have further evidence that POWER may be produced through friendly alliance of minds.

There is little if any doubt that Henry Ford is one of the best informed men in the business and industrial world. The question of his wealth needs no discussion. Analyze Mr Ford's intimate personal friends, some of whom have already been mentioned, and you will be prepared to understand the following statement: 'Men take on the nature and the habits and the POWER OF THOUGHT of those with whom they associate in a spirit of sympathy and harmony.'

Henry Ford whipped poverty, illiteracy, and ignorance by allying himself with great minds, whose vibrations of thought he absorbed into his own mind. Through his association with Edison, Burbank, Burroughs, and Firestone, Mr Ford added to his own brain power, the sum and substance of the intelligence, experience, knowledge, and spiritual forces of these four men. Moreover, he appropriated, and made use of the Master Mind principle through the methods of procedure described in this book.

This principle is available to you!

We have already mentioned Mahatma Gandhi. Perhaps the

majority of those who have heard of Gandhi, look upon him as merely an eccentric little man, who goes around without formal wearing apparel, and makes trouble for the British Government. In reality, Gandhi is not eccentric, but HE IS THE MOST POWERFUL MAN NOW LIVING. (Estimated by the number of his followers and their faith in their leader.) Moreover, he is probably the most powerful man who has ever lived. His power is passive, but it is real.

Let us study the method by which he attained his stupendous POWER. It may be explained in a few words. He came by POWER through inducing over two hundred million people to coordinate, with mind and body, in a spirit of HARMONY, for a DEFINITE PURPOSE.

In brief, Gandhi has accomplished a MIRACLE, for it is a miracle when two hundred million people can be induced—not forced—to cooperate in a spirit of HARMONY, for a limitless time. If you doubt that this is a miracle, try to induce ANY TWO PEOPLE to cooperate in a spirit of harmony for *any length of time*.

Every man who manages a business knows what a difficult matter it is to get employees to work together in a spirit even remotely resembling HARMONY.

The list of the chief sources from which POWER may be attained is, as you have seen, headed by INFINITE INTELLIGENCE. When two or more people coordinate in a spirit of HARMONY, and work toward a definite objective, they place themselves in position, through that alliance, to absorb power directly from the great universal storehouse of Infinite Intelligence. This is the greatest of all sources of POWER. It is the source to which the genius turns. It is the source to which every great leader turns, (whether he may be conscious of the fact or not). The other two major sources from which the knowledge, necessary for the accumulation of POWER, may be obtained are no more reliable than the five senses of man. The senses are not always reliable. Infinite Intelligence DOES NOT ERR.

In subsequent chapters, the methods by which Infinite Intelligence may be most readily contacted will be adequately described.

This is not a course on religion. No fundamental principle described in this book should be interpreted as being intended to interfere either directly, or indirectly, with any man's religious habits. This book has been confined, exclusively, to instructing the reader how to transmute the DEFINITE PURPOSE OF DESIRE FOR MONEY, into its monetary equivalent.

Read, THINK, and meditate as you read. Soon, the entire subject will unfold, and you will see it in perspective. You are now seeing the detail of the individual chapters.

Money is as shy and elusive as the 'old time' maiden. It must be wooed and won by methods not unlike those used by a determined lover, in pursuit of the girl of his choice. And, coincidental as it is, the POWER used in the 'wooing' of money is not greatly different from that used in wooing a maiden. That power, when successfully used in the pursuit of money must be mixed with FAITH. It must be mixed with DESIRE. It must be mixed with PERSISTENCE. It must be applied through a plan, and that plan must be set into ACTION.

When money comes in quantities known as 'the big money,' it flows to the one who accumulates it, as easily as water flows down hill. There exists a great unseen stream of POWER, which may be compared to a river; except that one side flows in one direction, carrying all who get into that side of the stream, onward and upward to WEALTH—and the other side flows in the opposite direction, carrying all who are unfortunate enough to get into it (and not able to extricate themselves from it), downward to misery and POVERTY.

Every man who has accumulated a great fortune, has recognized the existence of this stream of life. It consists of one's THINKING PROCESS. The positive emotions of thought form the side of the stream which carries one to fortune. The negative emotions form the side which carries one down to poverty.

This carries a thought of stupendous importance to the person who is following this book with the object of accumulating a fortune.

If you are in the side of the stream of POWER which leads to poverty, this may serve as an oar, by which you may propel yourself over into the other side of the stream. It can serve you ONLY through application and use. Merely reading, and passing judgment on it, either one way or another, will in no way benefit you.

Some people undergo the experience of alternating between the positive and negative sides of the stream, being at times on the positive side, and at times on the negative side. The Wall Street crash of '29 swept millions of people from the positive to the negative side of the stream. These millions are struggling, some of them in desperation and fear, to get back to the positive side of the stream. This book was written especially for those millions.

Poverty and riches often change places. The Crash taught

the world this truth, although the world will not long remember the lesson. Poverty may, and generally does, voluntarily take the place of riches. When riches take the place of poverty, the change is usually brought about through well conceived and carefully executed PLANS. Poverty needs no plan. It needs no one to aid it, because it is bold and ruthless. Riches are shy and timid. They have to be 'attracted.'

ANYBODY can WISH
for riches, and most
people do, but only a few
know that a definite plan,
plus a BURNING DESIRE
for wealth, are the only
dependable means of
accumulating wealth.

THE RICHEST MAN IN BABYLON

'A man's wealth is not in the coins he carries in his purse; it is the income he builds, the golden stream that continually flows into his purse and keeps it always bulging.' This 1926 classic serves as a talisman through its renowned collection of Babylonian parables for those seeking financial wisdom and stability in life. Its powerhouse of time-tested principles on how to gain and retain wealth has been inspiring readers for several generations now. A perfect guide to understand finances, it also discusses the 'five laws of gold' and provides us with insights on not only how to be in clover but also keep good luck at one's side. Even after almost 100 years of *The Richest Man in Babylon*, it continues to remain a classic bestseller.

4

THE RICHEST MAN IN BABYLON

In old Babylon there once lived a certain very rich man named Arkad. Far and wide he was famed for his great wealth. Also was be famed for his liberality. He was generous in his charities. He was generous with his family. He was liberal in his own expenses nevertheless each year his wealth increased more rapidly than he spent it.

And there were certain friends of younger days who came to him and said: "You, Arkad, are more fortunate than us. You have become the richest man in all Babylon while we struggle for existence. You can wear the finest garments and you can enjoy the rarest foods, while we must be content if we can clothe our families in raiment that is presentable and feed them as best we can.

"Yet, once we were equal. We studied under the same master. We played in the same games. And in neither the studies nor the games did you outshine us. And in the years since, you have been no more an honourable citizen than us.

"Nor have you worked harder or more faithfully, insofar as we can judge. Why, then, should a fickle fate single you out to enjoy all the good things of life and ignore us who are equally deserving?"

Thereupon Arkad remonstrated with them, saying, "If you have not acquired more than a bare existence in the years since we were youths, it is because you either have failed to learn the laws that govern the building of wealth, or else you do not observe them.

" 'Fickle Fate' is a vicious goddess who brings no permanent good to anyone. On the contrary, she brings ruin to almost every man upon whom she showers unearned gold. She makes wanton spenders, who soon dissipate all they receive and are left beset by overwhelming appetites and desires they have not the ability to gratify. Yet others whom she favours become misers and hoard their wealth, fearing to spend what they have, knowing they do not possess the ability to replace it. They further are beset by fear of robbers and doom themselves to lives of emptiness and secret misery.

"Others there probably are, who can take unearned gold and add to it and continue to be happy and contented citizens. But so few are they, I know of them but by hearsay. Think of the men you know who have inherited sudden wealth, and see if these things are not so.

" His friends admitted that of the men they knew who had inherited wealth these words were true, and they besought him to explain to them how he had become possessed of so much prosperity, so he continued: "In my youth I looked about me and saw all the good things there were to bring happiness and contentment. And I realized that wealth increased the potency of all these. "Wealth is a power. With wealth many things are possible.

"One may ornament the home with the richest of furnishings. One may sail the distant seas. One may feast on the delicacies of far lands.

One may buy the ornaments of the gold worker and the stone polisher.

One may even build mighty temples for the Gods.

One may do all these things and many others in which there is delight for the senses and gratification for the soul.

And, when I realized all this, I decided to myself that I would claim my share of the good things of life. I would not be one of those who stand afar off, enviously watching others enjoy. I would not be content to clothe myself in the cheapest raiment that looked respectable. I would not be satisfied with the lot of a poor man. On the contrary, I would make myself a guest at this banquet of good things.

"Being, as you know, the son of a humble merchant, one of a large family with no hope of an inheritance, and not being endowed, as you have so frankly said, with superior powers or wisdom, I decided that if I was to achieve what I desired, time and study would be required."

"As for time, all men have it in abundance. You, each of you, have let slip by sufficient time to have made yourselves wealthy. Yet, you admit; you have nothing to show except your good families, of which you can be justly proud.

As for study, did our wise teacher not teach us that learning was of two kinds: the one kind being the things we learned and knew, and the other being the training that taught us how to find out what we did not know?"

"Therefore I decided to find out how one might accumulate wealth, and when I had found out, to make this my task and do it well. For, is it not wise that we should enjoy while we dwell in the brightness of the sunshine, for sorrows enough shall descend upon us when we depart for the darkness of the world of spirit?"

"I found employment as a scribe in the hall of records, and long hours each day I laboured upon the clay tablets. Week after week, and month after month, I laboured, yet for my earnings I had naught to show. Food and clothing and penance to the gods, and other things of which I could remember not what, absorbed all my earnings. But my determination did not leave me.

And one day Algamish, the money lender, came to the house of the city master and ordered a copy of the Ninth Law, and he said to me, "I must have this in two days, and if the task is done by that time, two coppers will I give to thee."

So I laboured hard, but the law was long, and when Algamish returned the task was unfinished. He was angry, and had I been his slave, he would have beaten me. But knowing the city master would not permit him to injure me, I was unafraid, so I said to him, 'Algamish, you are a very rich man. Tell me how I may also become rich, and all night I will carve upon the clay, and when the sun rises it shall be completed.'

"He smiled at me and replied, 'You are a forward knave, but we will call it a bargain.'

All that night I carved, though my back pained and the smell of the wick made my head ache until my eyes could hardly see. However, when he returned at sunup, the tablets were complete."

" 'Now,' I said, 'tell me what you promised.'

" 'You have fulfilled your part of our bargain, my son,' he

said to me kindly, 'and I am ready to fulfill mine. I will tell you these things you wish to know because I am becoming an old man, and an old tongue loves to wag. And when youth comes to age for advice he receives the wisdom of years. But too often does youth think that age knows only the wisdom of days that are gone, and therefore profits not. But remember this, the sun that shines today is the sun that shone when thy father was born, and will still be shining when thy last grandchild shall pass into the darkness.'"

"'The thoughts of youth,' he continued, 'are bright lights that shine forth like the meteors that oft make brilliant the sky, but the wisdom of age is like the fixed stars that shine so unchanged that the sailor may depend upon them to steer his course.

"'Mark you well my words, for if you do not you will fail to grasp the truth that I will tell you, and you will think that your night's work has been in vain.'

Then he looked at me shrewdly from under his shaggy brows and said in a low, forceful tone,

'I found the road to wealth when I decided that a part of all I earned was mine to keep. And so will you.'

Then he continued to look at me with a glance that I could feel pierce me but said no more.

"'Is that all?' I asked.

"'That was sufficient to change the heart of a sheep herder into the heart of a money lender,' he replied.

"'But all I earn is mine to keep, is it not?' I demanded."

"'Far from it,' he replied. 'Do you not pay the garment-maker? Do you not pay the sandalmaker? Do you not pay for the things you eat? Can you live in Babylon without spending?

What have you to show for your earnings of the past mouth? What for the past year? Fool! You pay to everyone but yourself. Dullard, you labour for others. As well be a slave and work for what your master gives you to eat and wear. If you did keep for yourself one-tenth of all you earn, how much would you have in ten years?'"

"My knowledge of the numbers did not forsake me, and I answered, 'As much as I earn in one year.'"

"'You speak but half the truth,' he retorted. 'Every gold piece you save is a slave to work for you. Every copper it earns is its child that also can earn for you. If you would become wealthy, then what you save must earn, and its children must earn, that all may help to give to you the abundance you crave.'"

"'You think I cheat you for your long night's work,' he continued, 'but I am paying you a thousand times over if you have the intelligence to grasp the truth I offer you.'"

"'A part of all you earn is yours to keep. It should be not less than a tenth no matter how little you earn. It can be as much more as you can afford. Pay yourself first. Do not buy from the clothesmaker and the sandal-maker more than you can pay out of the rest and still have enough for food and charity and penance to the gods.

"'Wealth, like a tree, grows from a tiny seed. The first copper you save is the seed from which your tree of wealth shall grow. The sooner you plant that seed the sooner shall the tree grow. And the more faithfully you nourish and water that tree with consistent savings, the sooner may you bask in contentment beneath its shade.'"

"So saying, he took his tablets and went away."

"I thought much about what he had said to me, and it

seemed reasonable. So I decided that I would try it. Each time I was paid I took one from each ten pieces of copper and hid it away. And strange as it may seem, I was no shorter of funds, than before. I noticed little difference as I managed to get along without it. But often I was tempted, as my hoard began to grow, to spend it for some of the good things the merchants displayed, brought by camels and ships from the land of the Phoenicians.

But I wisely refrained.

A twelfth month after Algamish had gone he again returned and told me, 'Son, have you paid to yourself not less than one-tenth of all you have earned for the past year?'"

"I answered proudly, 'Yes, master, I have.' " 'That is good,' he answered beaming upon me, 'and what have you done with it?'

" 'I have given it to Azmur, the brickmaker, who told me that he was traveling over the far seas and in Tyre he would buy for me the rare jewels of the Phoenicians. When he returns we shall sell these at high prices and divide the earnings.' "

" 'Every fool must learn,' he growled, 'but why trust the knowledge of a brickmaker about jewels? Would you go to the breadmaker to inquire about the stars? No, by my tunic, you would go to the astrologer, if you had power to think. Your savings are gone, youth, you have jerked your wealth tree up by the roots. But plant another. Try again. And next time if you would have advice about jewels, go to the jewel merchant. If you would know the truth about sheep, go to the herdsman. Advice is one thing that is freely given away, but watch that you take only what is worth having. He who takes advice about his savings from one who is inexperienced in such matters, shall pay with his savings for proving the falsity of their opinions.' Saying this, he went away."

"And it was as he said. For the Phoenicians are scoundrels and sold to Azmur worthless bits of glass that looked like gems. But as Algamish had bid me, I again saved each tenth copper, for I now had formed the habit and it was no longer difficult.

"Again, twelve months later, Algamish came to the room of the scribes and addressed me.

'What progress have you made since last I saw you?'"

"'I have paid myself faithfully,' I replied, 'and my savings I have entrusted to Agger the shieldmaker, to buy bronze, and each fourth month he does pay me the rental.'"

"'That is good. And what do you do with the rental?' "'I do have a great feast with honey and fine wine and spiced cake. Also I have bought me a scarlet tunic. And some day I shall buy me a young ass upon which to ride.' "To which Algamish laughed, 'You do eat the children of your savings. Then how do you expect them to work for you? And how can they have children that will also work for you? First get thee an army of golden slaves and then many a rich banquet may you enjoy without regret.' So saying he again went away."

"I did not again see him for two years, when he once more returned and his face was full of deep lines and his eyes drooped, for he was becoming a very old man. And he said to me, 'Arkad, hast thou yet achieved the wealth thou dreamed of?'"

"And I answered, 'Not yet all that I desire, but some I have and it earns more, and its earnings earn more.'"

"'And do you still take the advice of brickmakers?'"

"'About brickmaking they give good advice,' I retorted.

"'Arkad,' he continued, 'you have learned your lessons well. You first learned to live upon less than you could earn. Next you learned to seek advice from those who were competent through their own experiences to give it. And, lastly, you have learned to make gold work for you."

"'You have taught yourself how to acquire money, how to keep it, and how to use it. Therefore, you are competent for a responsible position. I am becoming an old man. My sons think only of spending and give no thought to earning. My interests are great and I fear too much for me to look after. If you will go to Nippur and look after my lands there, I shall make you my partner and you shall share in my estate.'"

"So I went to Nippur and took charge of his holdings, which were large. And because I was full of ambition and because I had mastered the three laws of successfully handling wealth, I was enabled to increase greatly the value of his properties.

So I prospered much, and when the spirit of Algamish departed for the sphere of darkness, I did share in his estate as he had arranged under the law. So spake Arkad, and when he had finished his tale, one of his friends said, 'You were indeed fortunate that Algamish made of you an heir.'"

"Fortunate only in that I had the desire to prosper before I first met him. For four years did I not prove my definiteness of purpose by keeping one-tenth of all earnings? Would you call a fisherman lucky who for years so studied the habits of the fish that with each changing wind he could cast his nets about them? Opportunity is a haughty goddess who wastes no time with those who are unprepared."

"You had strong will power to keep on after you lost your first year's savings. You are unusual in that way," spoke up another.

"Will power!" retorted Arkad. "What nonsense. Do you think will power gives a man the strength to lift a burden the camel cannot carry, or to draw a load the oxen cannot budge?

Will power is but the unflinching purpose to carry a task you set for yourself to fulfillment. If I set for myself a task, be it ever so trifling, I shall see it through. How else shall I have confidence in myself to do important things? Should I say to myself, 'For a hundred days as I walk across the bridge into the city, I will pick from the road a pebble and cast it into the stream,' I would do it. If on the seventh day I passed by without remembering, I would not say to myself'—Tomorrow I will cast two pebbles which will do as well.' Instead, I would retrace my steps and cast the pebble. Nor on the twentieth day would I say to myself, 'Arkad, this is useless. What does it avail you to cast a pebble every day? Throw in a handful and be done with it.' No, I would not say that nor do it. When I set a task for myself, I complete it. Therefore, I am careful not to start difficult and impractical tasks, because I love leisure."

And then another friend spoke up and said, "If what you tell is true, and it does seem as you have said, reasonable, then being so simple, if all men did it, there would not be enough wealth to go around."

"Wealth grows wherever men exert energy," Arkad replied. "If a rich man builds him a new palace, is the gold he pays out gone? No, the brickmaker has part of it and the labourer has part of it, and the artist has part of it. And everyone who labours upon the house has part of it Yet when the palace is ompleted, is it not worth all it cost? And is the ground upon which it stands not worth more because it is there? And is the ground that adjoins it not worth more because it is there? Wealth grows in magic ways. No man can prophesy the limit of it. Have not the Phoenicians built great cities on barren coasts with the wealth that comes from their ships of commerce on the seas?"

"What then do you advise us to do that we also may become rich?" asked still another of his friends. "The years have passed and we are no longer young men and we have nothing put by."

"I advise that you take the wisdom of Algamish and say to yourselves, 'A part of all I earn is mine to keep.' Say it in the morning when you first arise. Say it at noon. Say it at night. Say it each hour of every day. Say it to yourself until the words stand out like letters of fire across the sky."

"Impress yourself with the idea. Fill yourself with the thought. Then take whatever portion seems wise. Let it be not less than one-tenth and lay it by. Arrange your other expenditures to do this if necessary. But lay by that portion first. Soon you will realize what a rich feeling it is to own a treasure upon which you alone have claim. As it grows it will stimulate you. A new joy of life will thrill you. Greater efforts will come to you to earn more. For of your increased earnings, will not the same percentage be also yours to keep?"

"Then learn to make your treasure work for you. Make it your slave. Make its children and its children's children work for you."

"Insure an income for thy future. Look thou at the aged and forget not that in the days to come thou also will be numbered among them. Therefore invest thy treasure with greatest caution that it be not lost. Usurious rates of return are deceitful sirens that sing but to lure the unwary upon the rocks of loss and remorse."

"Provide also that thy family may not want should the Gods call thee to their realms. For such protection it is always possible to make provision with small payments at regular intervals. Therefore the provident man delays not in expectation of a large sum becoming available for such a wise purpose.

"Counsel with wise men. Seek the advice of men whose daily work is handling money. Let them save you from such an error as I myself made in entrusting my money to the judgment of Azmur, the brickmaker. A small return and a safe one is far more desirable than risk."

"Enjoy life while you are here. Do not overstrain or try to save too much. If one-tenth of all you earn is as much as you can comfortably keep, be content to keep this portion. Live otherwise according to your income and let not yourself get niggardly and afraid to spend. Life is good and life is rich with things worthwhile and things to enjoy."

His friends thanked him and went away. Some were silent because they had no imagination and could not understand. Some were sarcastic because they thought that one so rich should divide with old friends who are not so fortunate. But some had in their eyes a new light. They realized that Algamish had returned to the room of the scribes each time because he was watching a man work his way out of darkness into light. When that man had found the light, a place awaited him. No one could fill that place until he had for himself worked out his own understanding, until he was ready for opportunity.

These latter were the ones, who, in the following years, frequently revisited Arkad, who received them gladly. He counseled with them and gave them his wisdom freely-as men of broad experience are always glad to do. He assisted them in investing their savings in a manner that it would bring in a good interest with safety and would neither be lost nor entangled in investments that paid no dividends.

The turning point in these men's lives came upon that day

when they realized the truth that had come from Algamish to Arkad and from Arkad to them.

A PART OF ALL YOU EARN
IS YOURS TO KEEP.

5

SEVEN CURES FOR A LEAN PURSE

The glory of Babylon endures. Down through the ages its reputation comes to us as the richest of cities, its treasures as fabulous.

Yet it was not always so. The riches of Babylon were the results of the wisdom of its people. They first had to learn how to become wealthy.

When the Good King, Sargon, returned to Babylon after defeating his enemies, the Elamites, he was confronted with a serious situation. The Royal Chancellor explained it to the King thus:

"After many years of great prosperity brought to our people because your majesty built the great irrigation canals and the mighty temples of the Gods, now that these works are completed the people seem unable to support themselves."

"The labourers are without employment. The merchants have few customers. The farmers are unable to sell their produce. The people have not enough gold to buy food."

"But where has all the gold gone that we spent for these

great improvements?" demanded the King.

"It has found its way, I fear," responded the Chancellor, "into the possession of a few very rich men of our city. It filtered through the fingers of most our people as quickly as the goat's milk goes through the strainer. Now that the stream of gold has ceased to flow, most of our people have nothing to for their earnings."

The King was thoughtful for some time. Then he asked, "Why should so few men be able to acquire all the gold?"

"Because they know how," replied the Chancellor. "One may not condemn a man for succeeding because he knows how. Neither may one with justice take away from a man what he has fairly earned, to give to men of less ability."

"But why," demanded the King, "should not all the people learn how to accumulate gold and therefore become themselves rich and prosperous?"

"Quite possible, your excellency. But who can teach them? Certainly not the priests, because they know naught of money making."

"Who knows best in all our city how to become wealthy, Chancellor?" asked the King.

"Thy question answers itself, your majesty. Who has amassed the greatest wealth, in Babylon?"

"Well said, my able Chancellor. It is Arkad. He is richest man in Babylon. Bring him before me on the morrow."

Upon the following day, as the King had decreed, Arkad appeared before him, straight and sprightly despite his three score years and ten.

"Arkad," spoke the King, "is it true thou art the richest man in Babylon?"

"So it is reported, your majesty, and no man disputes it"

"How becamest thou so wealthy?"

"By taking advantage of opportunities available to all citizens of our good city."

"Thou hadst nothing to start with?"

"Only a great desire for wealth. Besides this, nothing."

"Arkad," continued the King, "our city is in a very unhappy state because a few men know how to acquire wealth and therefore monopolize it, while the mass of our citizens lack the knowledge of how to keep any part of the gold they receive."

"It is my desire that Babylon be the wealthiest city in the world. Therefore, it must be a city of many wealthy men. Therefore, we must teach all the people how to acquire riches. Tell me, Arkad, is there any secret to acquiring wealth? Can it be taught?"

"It is practical, your majesty. That which one man knows can be taught to others."

The king's eyes glowed. "Arkad, thou speaketh the words I wish to hear. Wilt thou lend thyself to this great cause? Wilt thou teach thy knowledge to a school for teachers, each of whom shall teach others until there are enough trained to teach these truths to every worthy subject in my domain?"

Arkad bowed and said, "I am thy humble servant to command. Whatever knowledge I possess will I gladly give for the betterment of my fellowmen and the glory of my King. Let your good chancellor arrange for me a class of one hundred men and I will teach to them those seven cures which did fatten my purse, than which there was none leaner in all Babylon."

A fortnight later, in compliance with the King's command, the chosen hundred assembled in the great hall of the Temple of Learning, seated upon colourful rings in a semicircle. Arkad sat beside a small taboret upon which smoked a sacred lamp sending forth a strange and pleasing odor.

"Behold the richest man in Babylon," whispered a student, nudging his neighbor as Arkad arose. "He is but a man even as the rest of us."

"As a dutiful subject of our great King," Arkad began, "I stand before you in his service. Because once I was a poor youth who did greatly desire gold, and because I found knowledge that enabled me to acquire it, he asks that I impart unto you my knowledge."

"I started my fortune in the humblest way. I had no advantage not enjoyed as fully by you and every citizen in Babylon."

"The first storehouse of my treasure was a well-purse. I loathed its useless emptiness. I desired it be round and full, clinking with the sound of gold. Therefore, I sought every remedy for a lean purse. I found seven."

"To you, who are assembled before me, shall I explain the seven cures for a lean purse which I do recommend to all men who desire much gold. Each day for seven days will I explain to you one of the seven remedies."

"Listen attentively to the knowledge that I will impart. Debate it with me. Discuss it among yourselves. Learn these lessons thoroughly, that ye may also plant in your own purse the seed of wealth. First must each of you start wisely to build a fortune of his own. Then wilt thou be competent, and only then, to teach these truths to others.

"I shall teach to you in simple ways how to fatten your purses. This is the first step leading to the temple of wealth, and no man may climb who cannot plant his feet firmly upon the first step.

"We shall now consider the first cure."

THE FIRST CURE

Start thy purse to fattening

Arkad addressed a thoughtful man in the second row. "My good friend, at what craft workest thou?"

"I," replied the man, "am a scribe and carve records upon the clay tablets." "Even at such labour did I myself earn my first coppers. Therefore, thou hast the same opportunity to build a fortune."

He spoke to a florid-faced man, farther back. "Pray tell also what dost thou to earn thy bread?"

"I," responded this man, "am a meat butcher. I do buy the goats, the farmers raise, and kill them, and sell the meat to the housewives and the hides to the sandal makers."

"Because thou dost also labour and earn, thou hast every advantage to succeed that I did possess."

In this way did Arkad proceed to find out how each man laboured to earn his living. When he had done questioning them, he said:

"Now, my students, ye can see that there are many trades and labours at which men may earn coins. Each of the ways of earning is a stream of gold from which the worker doth divert by his labours a portion to his own purse. Therefore into the purse of each of you flows a stream of coins-large or small, according to his ability. Is it not so?"

Thereupon they agreed that it was so. "Then," continued

Arkad, "if each of you desireth to build for yourselves a fortune, is it not wise to start by utilizing that source of wealth which has been already established?"

To this they agreed.

Then Arkad turned to a humble man who had declared himself an egg merchant. "If thou select one of thy baskets and put into it each morning ten eggs and take out from it each evening nine eggs, what will eventually happen?"

"It will become in time overflowing."

"Why?"

"Because each day I put in one more egg than I take out."

Arkad turned to the class with a smile. "Does any man here have a lean purse?"

First they looked amused. Then they laughed. Lastly they waved their purses in jest.

"All right," he continued, "Now I shall tell thee the first remedy I learned to cure a lean purse. Do exactly as I have suggested to the egg merchant. For every ten coins thou placest within thy purse take out for use but nine. Thy purse will start to fatten at once and its increasing weight will feel good in thy hand and bring satisfaction to thy soul."

"Deride not what I say because of its simplicity. Truth is always simple. I told thee I would tell how built my fortune. This was my beginning. I, too, carried a lean purse and cursed it because there was naught within to satisfy my desires. But when I began to take out from my purse but nine parts of ten I put in, it began to fatten. So will thine."

"Now I will tell a strange truth, the reason for which I know not. When I ceased to pay out more than nine-tenths of my earnings, I managed to get along just as well. I was not shorter than before. Also, ere long, did coins come to me more easily than before. Surely it is a law of the Gods that unto him who keepeth and spendeth not a certain part of all his earnings, shall gold come more easily. Likewise, him whose purse is empty does gold avoid."

"Which desirest thou the most? Is it the gratification of thy desires of each day, a jewel, a bit of finery, better raiment, more food; things quickly gone and forgotten? Or is it substantial belongings, gold, lands, herds, merchandise, income-bringing investments? The coins thou takest from thy purse bring the first. The coins thou leavest within it will bring the latter."

"This, my students, was the first cure I did discover for my lean purse: 'For each ten coins I put in, to spend but nine.' Debate this amongst yourselves. If any man proves it untrue, tell me upon the morrow when we shall meet again."

THE SECOND CURE

Control thy expenditures

"Some of your members, my students, have asked me this: How can a man keep one-tenth of all he earns in his purse when all the coins he earns are not enough for his necessary expenses?" So did Arkad address his students upon the second day.

"Yesterday how many of thee carried lean purses?"

"All of us," answered the class.

"Yet, thou do not all earn the same. Some earn much more than others. Some have much larger families to support. Yet, all purses were equally lean. Now I will tell thee an unusual truth about men and sons of men. It is this; That what each of us calls our 'necessary expenses' will always grow to equal our incomes unless we protest to the contrary."

"Confuse not the necessary expenses with thy desires. Each of you, together with your good families, have more desires than your earnings can gratify. Therefore are thy earnings spent to gratify these desires insofar as they will go. Still thou retainest many ungratified desires."

"All men are burdened with more desires than they can gratify. Because of my wealth thinkest thou I may gratify every desire? 'Tis a false idea. There are limits to my time. There are limits to my strength. There are limits to the distance I may travel. There are limits to what I may eat. There are limits to the zest with which I may enjoy."

"I say to you that just as weeds grow in a field wherever the farmer leaves space for their roots, even so freely do desires grow in men whenever there is a possibility of them being gratified. Thy desires are a multitude and those that thou mayest gratify are but few."

"Study thoughtfully thy accustomed habits of living. Herein may be most often found certain accepted expenses that may wisely be reduced or eliminated. Let thy motto be one hundred percent of appreciated value demanded for each coin spent."

"Therefore, engrave upon the clay each thing for which thou desireth to spend. Select those that are necessary and others that are possible through the expenditure of nine- tenths of thy income. Cross out the rest and consider them but a part of that great multitude of desires that must go unsatisfied and regret them not."

"Budget then thy necessary expenses. Touch not the one-tenth that is fattening thy purse. Let this be thy great desire that is being fulfilled. Keep working with thy budget, keep adjusting it to help thee. Make it thy first assistant in defending thy fattening purse."

Hereupon one of the students, wearing a robe of red and gold, arose and said, "I am a free man. I believe that it is my right to enjoy the good things of life. Therefore do I rebel against the slavery of a budget which determines just how much I may spend and for what. I feel it would take much pleasure from my life and make me little more than a pack-ass to carry a burden."

To him Arkad replied, "Who, my friend, would determine thy budget?"

"I would make it for myself," responded the protesting one.

"In that case were a pack-ass to budget his burden would he include therein jewels and rugs and heavy bars of gold? Not so. He would include hay and grain and a bag of water for the desert trail."

"The purpose of a budget is to help thy purse to fatten. It is to assist thee to have thy necessities and, insofar as attainable, thy other desires. It is to enable thee to realize thy most cherished desires by defending them from thy casual wishes. Like a bright light in a dark cave thy budget shows the leaks from thy purse and enables thee to stop them and control thy expenditures for definite and gratifying purposes."

"This, then, is the second cure for a lean purse. *Budget thy expenses that thou mayest have coins to pay for thy necessities, to pay for thy enjoyments and to gratify thy worthwhile desires without spending more than nine-tenths of thy earnings.*"

THE THIRD CURE
Make thy gold multiply

"Behold! Thy lean purse is fattening. Thou hast disciplined thyself to leave therein one-tenth of all thou earneth. Thou hast controlled thy expenditures to protect thy growing treasure. Next, we will consider means to put thy treasure to labour and to increase. Gold in a purse is gratifying to own and satisfieth a miserly soul but earns nothing. The gold we may retain from our earnings is but the start. The earnings it will make shall build our fortunes." So spoke Arkad upon the third day to his class.

"How therefore may we put our gold to work? My first investment was unfortunate, for I lost all. Its tale I will relate later. My first profitable investment was a loan I made to a man named Aggar, a shield maker. Once each year did he buy large shipments of bronze brought from across the sea to use in his trade. Lacking sufficient capital to pay the merchants, he would borrow from those who had extra coins. He was an honourable man. His borrowing he would repay, together with a liberal rental, as he sold his shields."

"Each time I loaned to him I loaned back also the rental he had paid to me. Therefore not only did my capital increase, but its earnings likewise increased. Most gratifying was it to have these sums return to my purse."

"I tell you, my students, a man's wealth is not in the coins he carries in his purse; it is the income he buildeth, the golden stream that continually floweth into his purse and keepeth it always bulging. That is what every man desireth. That is what thou, each one of thee desireth; an income that continueth to come whether thou work or travel."

"Great income I have acquired. So great that I am called a very rich man. My loans to Aggar were my first training in profitable investment. Gaining wisdom from this experience, I extended my loans and investments as my capital increased. From a few sources at first, from many sources later, flowed into my purse a golden stream of wealth available for such wise uses as I should decide."

"Behold, from my humble earnings I had begotten a hoard of golden slaves, each labouring and earning more gold. As they laboured for me, so their children also laboured and their children's children until great was the income from their combined efforts.

"Gold increaseth rapidly when making reasonable earnings as thou wilt see from the following: A farmer, when his first son was born, took ten pieces of silver to a money lender and asked him to keep it on rental for his son until he became twenty years of age. This the money lender did, and agreed the rental should be one-fourth of its value each four years. The farmer asked, because this sum he had set aside as belonging to his son, that the rental be add to the principal."

"When the boy had reached the age of twenty years, the farmer again went to the money lender to inquire about the silver. The money lender explained that because this sum had been increased by compound interest, the original ten pieces of silver had now grown to thirty and one-half pieces."

"The farmer was well pleased and because the son did not need the coins, he left them with the money lender. When the son became fifty years of age, the father meantime having passed to the other world, the money lender paid the son in settlement one hundred and sixty-seven pieces of silver."

"Thus in fifty years had the investment multiplied itself at rental almost seventeen times. "This, then, is the third cure for a lean purse: to put each coin to labouring that it may reproduce its kind even as the flocks of the field and help bring to thee income, a stream of wealth that shall flow constantly into thy purse."

THE FOURTH CURE
Guard thy treasures from loss

"Misfortune loves a shining mark. Gold in a man's purse must be guarded with firmness, else it be lost. Thus it is wise that we must first secure small amounts and learn to protect them before the Gods entrust us with larger." So spoke Arkad upon the fourth day to his class.

"Every owner of gold is tempted by opportunities whereby it would seem that he could make large sums by its investment in most plausible projects. Often friends and relatives eagerly enter such investment and urge him to follow.

"The first sound principle of investment is security for thy principal. Is it wise to be intrigued by larger earnings when thy principal may be lost? I say not. The penalty of risk is probable loss. Study carefully, before parting with thy treasure, each assurance that it may be safely reclaimed. Be not misled by thine own romantic desires to make wealth rapidly."

"Before thou loan it to any man assure thyself of his ability to repay and his reputation for doing so, that thou mayest not unwittingly be making him a present of thy hard-earned treasure."

"Before thou entrust it as an investment in any field, acquaint thyself with the dangers which may beset it."

"My own first investment was a tragedy to me at the time. The guarded savings of a year I did entrust to a brickmaker, named Azmur, who was traveling over the far seas and in Tyre agreed to buy for me the rare jewels of the Phoenicians. These we would sell upon his return and divide the profits.

The Phoenicians were scoundrels and sold him bits of glass. My treasure was lost. Today, my training would show to me at once the folly of entrusting a brickmaker to buy jewels."

"Therefore, do I advise thee from the wisdom of my experiences: be not too confident of thine own wisdom in entrusting thy treasures to the possible pitfalls of investments. Better by far to consult the wisdom of those experienced in handling money for profit. Such advice is freely given for the asking and may readily possess a value equal in gold to the sum thou considerest investing. In truth, such is its actual value if it save thee from loss."

"This, then, is the fourth cure for a lean purse, and of great importance if it prevent thy purse from being emptied once it has become well filled. Guard thy treasure from loss by investing only where thy principal is safe, where it may be reclaimed if desirable, and where thou will not fail to collect a fair rental. Consult with wise men. Secure the advice of those experienced in the profitable handling of gold. Let their wisdom protect thy treasure from unsafe investments."

THE FIFTH CURE

Make of thy dwelling a profitable investment

"If a man setteth aside nine parts of his earnings to live and enjoy life, and if any part of this nine parts he can turn into a profitable investment without detriment to his wellbeing, then so much faster will his treasures grow." So spake Arkad to his class at their fifth lesson.

"All too many of our men of Babylon do raise their families in unseemly quarters. They do pay to exacting landlords liberal rentals for rooms where their wives have not a spot to raise the blooms that gladden a woman's heart and their children have no place to play their games except in the unclean alleys."

"No man's family can fully enjoy life unless they do have a plot of ground wherein children can play in the clean earth and where the wife may raise not only blossoms but good rich herbs to feed her family."

"To a man's heart it brings gladness to eat the figs from his own trees and the grapes of his own vines. To own his own domicile and to have a place he is proud to care for, putteth confidence in his heart and greater effort behind all his endeavors. Therefore, do I recommend that every man own the roof that sheltereth him and his."

"Nor is it beyond the ability of any well intentioned man to own his home. Hath not our great king so widely extended the walls of Babylon that within them much land is now unused and may be purchased at sums most reasonable?"

"Also I say to you, my students, that the money lenders gladly consider the desires of men who seek homes and land for their families. Readily may thou borrow to pay the brickmaker and the builder for such commendable purposes, if thou can show a reasonable portion of the necessary sum which thou thyself hath provided for the purpose."

"Then when the house be built, thou canst pay the money lender with the same regularity as thou didst pay the landlord.

Because each payment will reduce thy indebtedness to the money lender, a few years will satisfy his loan.

"Then will thy heart be glad because thou wilt own in thy own right a valuable property and thy only cost will be the king's taxes."

"Also wilt thy good wife go more often to the river to wash thy robes, that each time returning she may bring a goatskin of water to pour upon the growing things."

"Thus come many blessings to the man who owneth his own house. And greatly will it reduce his cost of living, making available more of his earnings for pleasures and the gratification of his desires. This, then, is the fifth cure for a lean purse: Own thy own home"

THE SIXTH CURE

Insure a future income

"The life of every man proceedeth from his childhood to his old age. This is the path of life and no man may deviate from it unless the Gods call him prematurely to the world beyond. Therefore do I say that it behooves a man to make preparation for a suitable income in the days to come, when he is no longer young, and to make preparations for his family should he be no longer with them to comfort and support them. This lesson shall instruct thee in providing a full purse when time has made thee less able to learn." So Arkad addressed his class upon the sixth day.

"The man who, because of his understanding of the laws of wealth, acquireth a growing surplus, should give thought to those future days. He should plan certain investments or provision that may endure safely for many years, yet will be available when the time arrives which he has so wisely anticipated.

"There are diverse ways by which a man may provide with safety for his future. He may provide a hiding place and there bury a secret treasure. Yet, no matter with what skill it be hidden, it may nevertheless become the loot of thieves. For this reason I recommend not this plan.

"A man may buy houses or lands for this purpose. If wisely chosen as to their usefulness and value in the future, they are permanent in their value and their earnings or their sale will provide well for his purpose.

"A man may loan a small sum to the money lender and increase it at regular periods. The rental which the money lender adds to this will largely add to its increase. I do know a sandal maker, named Ansan, who explained to me not long ago that each week for eight years he had deposited with his money lender two pieces of silver. The money lender had but recently given him an accounting over which he greatly rejoiced. The total of his small deposits with their rental at the customary rate of one-fourth their value for each four years, had now become a thousand and forty pieces of silver.

"I did gladly encourage him further by demonstrating to him with my knowledge of the numbers that in twelve years more, if he would keep his regular deposits of but two pieces of silver each week, the money lender would then owe him four thousand pieces of silver, a worthy competence for the rest of his life.

"Surely, when such a small payment made with regularity doth produce such profitable results, no man can afford not to insure a treasure for his old age and the protection of his family, no matter how prosperous his business and his investments may be.

"I would that I might say more about this. In my mind rests a belief that some day wisethinking men will devise a plan to insure against death whereby many men pay in but a trifling sum regularly, the aggregate making a handsome sum for the family of each member who passeth to the beyond. This do I see as something desirable and which I could highly recommend.

But today it is not possible because it must reach beyond the life of any man or any partnership to operate. It must be as stable as the King's throne. Some day do I feel that such a plan shall come to pass and be a great blessing to many men, because even the first small payment will make available a snug fortune for the family of a member should he pass on.

"But because we live in our own day and not in the days which are to come, must we take advantage of those means and ways of accomplishing our purposes. Therefore do I recommend to all men, that they, by wise and well thought out methods, do provide against a lean purse in their mature years. For a lean purse to a man no longer able to earn or to a family without its head is a sore tragedy.

"This, then, is the sixth cure for a lean purse. Provide in advance for the needs of thy growing age and the protection of thy family."

THE SEVENTH CURE

Increase thy ability to earn

"This day do I speak to thee, my students, of one of the most vital remedies for a lean purse. Yet, I will talk not of gold but of yourselves, of the men beneath the robes of many colours who do sit before me. I will talk to you of those things within the minds and lives of men which do work for or against their success." So did Arkad address his class upon the seventh day.

"Not long ago came to me a young man seeking to borrow. When I questioned him the cause of his necessity, he complained that his earnings were insufficient to pay his expenses. Thereupon I explained to him, this being the case, he was a poor customer for the money lender, as he possessed no surplus earning capacity to repay the loan."

" 'What you need, young man,' I told him, 'is to earn more coins. What dost thou to increase thy capacity to earn?' "

" 'All that I can do' he replied. 'Six times within two moons have I approached my master to request that my pay be increased, but without success. No man can go oftener than that.' "

"We may smile at his simplicity, yet he did possess one of the vital requirements to increase his earnings. Within him was a strong desire to earn more, a proper and commendable desire.

"Preceding accomplishment must be desire. Thy desires must be strong and definite. General desires are but weak longings. For a man to wish to be rich is of little purpose. For a man to desire five pieces of gold is a tangible desire which he can press to fulfillment. After he has backed his desire for five pieces of gold with strength of purpose to secure it, next he can find similar ways to obtain ten pieces and then twenty pieces and later a thousand pieces and, behold, he has become wealthy. In learning to secure his one definite small desire, he hath trained himself to secure a larger one. This is the process by which wealth is accumulated: first in small sums, then in larger ones as a man learns and becomes more capable."

"Desires must be simple and definite. They defeat their own purpose should they be too many, too confusing, or beyond a man's training to accomplish."

As a man perfecteth himself in his calling even so doth his ability to earn increase. In those days when I was a humble scribe carving upon the clay for a few coppers each day, I observed that other workers did more than I and were paid more. Therefore, did I determine that I would be exceeded by none. Nor did it take long for me to discover the reason for their greater success. More interest in my work, more concentration upon my task, more persistence in my effort, and, behold, few men could carve more tablets in a day than I. With reasonable promptness my increased skill was rewarded, nor was it necessary for me to go six times to my master to request recognition."

"The more of wisdom we know, the more we may earn. That man who seeks to learn more of his craft shall be richly rewarded. If he is an artisan, he may seek to learn the methods and the tools of those most skillful in the same line. If he laboureth at the law or at healing, he may consult and exchange knowledge with others of his calling. If he be a merchant, he may continually seek better goods that can be purchased at lower prices."

"Always do the affairs of man change and improve because keen-minded men seek greater skill that they may better serve those upon whose patronage they depend. Therefore, I urge all men to be in the front rank of progress and not to stand still, lest they be left behind. "Many things come to make a man's life rich with gainful experiences. Such things as the following, a man must do if he respects himself:

"He must pay his debts with all the promptness within his

power, not purchasing that for which he is unable to pay."

"He must take care of his family that they may think and speak well of him."

"He must make a will of record that, in case the Gods call him, proper and honourable division of his property be accomplished."

"He must have compassion upon those who are injured and smitten by misfortune and aid them within reasonable limits." He must do deeds of thoughtfulness to those dear to him."

"Thus the seventh and last remedy for a lean purse is to cultivate thy own powers, to study and become wiser, to become more skillful, to so act as to respect thyself. Thereby shalt thou acquire confidence in thyself to achieve thy carefully considered desires."

"These then are the seven cures for a lean purse, which, out of the experience of a long and successful life, I do urge for all men who desire wealth. "There is more gold in Babylon, my students, than thou dreamest of. There is abundance for all."

"Go thou forth and practice these truths that thou mayest prosper and grow wealthy, as is thy right."

"Go thou forth and teach these truths that every honourable subject of his majesty may also share liberally in the ample wealth of our beloved city."

THERE IS A SCIENCE OF GETTING RICH

In the international bestseller book, *The Science of Getting Rich*, Wallace D. Wattles provides us with a unique practical guide to achieving economic and emotional security in our lives. He provides us with practical principles which are embedded in science and philosophy, and a plan of action that will help create a harmonious environment for ourselves, complete with wealth, wisdom and happiness.

6

THERE IS A SCIENCE OF GETTING RICH

There is a Science of getting rich, and it is an exact science, like algebra or arithmetic. There are certain laws which govern the process of acquiring riches; once these laws are learned and obeyed by any man, he will get rich with mathematical certainty.

The ownership of money and property comes as a result of doing things in a certain way; those who do things in this Certain Way, whether on purpose or accidentally, get rich; while those who do not do things in this Certain Way, no matter how hard they work or how able they are, remain poor.

It is a natural law that like causes always produce like effects; and, therefore, any man or woman who learns to do things in this certain way will infallibly get rich.

That the above statement is true is shown by the following facts:

Getting rich is not a matter of environment, for, if it were, all the people in certain neighborhoods would become wealthy; the people of one city would all be rich, while those of other towns would all be poor; or the inhabitants of one state would roll in wealth, while those of an adjoining state would be in poverty.

But everywhere we see rich and poor living side by side, in the same environment, and often engaged in the same vocations. When two men are in the same locality, and in the same business, and one gets rich while the other remains poor, it shows that getting rich is not, primarily, a matter of environment. Some environments may be more favorable than others, but when two men in the same business are in the same neighborhood, and one gets rich while the other fails, it indicates that getting rich is the result of doing things in a Certain Way.

And further, the ability to do things in this certain way is not due solely to the possession of talent, for many people who have great talent remain poor, while other who have very little talent get rich.

Studying the people who have got rich, we find that they are an average lot in all respects, having no greater talents and abilities than other men. It is evident that they do not get rich because they possess talents and abilities that other men have not, but because they happen to do things in a Certain Way.

Getting rich is not the result of saving, or "thrift"; many very penurious people are poor, while free spenders often get rich.

Nor is getting rich due to doing things which others fail to do; for two men in the same business often do almost exactly the same things, and one gets rich while the other remains poor or becomes bankrupt.

From all these things, we must come to the conclusion that getting rich is the result of doing things in a Certain Way.

If getting rich is the result of doing things in a Certain Way, and if like causes always produce like effects, then any man or woman who can do things in that way can become rich, and the whole matter is brought within the domain of exact science.

The question arises here, whether this Certain Way may not be so difficult that only a few may follow it. This cannot be true, as we have seen, so far as natural ability is concerned. Talented people get rich, and blockheads get rich; intellectually brilliant people get rich, and very stupid people get rich; physically strong people get rich, and weak and sickly people get rich.

Some degree of ability to think and understand is, of course, essential; but in so far natural ability is concerned, any man or woman who has sense enough to read and understand these words can certainly get rich.

Also, we have seen that it is not a matter of environment. Location counts for something; one would not go to the heart of the Sahara and expect to do successful business.

Getting rich involves the necessity of dealing with men, and of being where there are people to deal with; and if these people are inclined to deal in the way you want to deal, so much the better. But that is about as far as environment goes.

If anybody else in your town can get rich, so can you; and if anybody else in your state can get rich, so can you.

Again, it is not a matter of choosing some particular business or profession. People get rich in every business, and in every profession; while their next-door neighbors in the same vocation remain in poverty.

It is true that you will do best in a business which you like, and which is congenial to you; and if you have certain talents which are well developed, you will do best in a business which calls for the exercise of those talents.

Also, you will do best in a business which is suited to your locality; an ice-cream parlor would do better in a warm climate than in Greenland, and a salmon fishery will succeed better in the Northwest than in Florida, where there are no salmon.

But, aside from these general limitations, getting rich is not dependent upon your engaging in some particular business, but upon your learning to do things in a Certain Way. If you are now in business, and anybody else in your locality is getting rich in the same business, while you are not getting rich, it is because you are not doing things in the same Way that the other person is doing them.

No one is prevented from getting rich by lack of capital. True, as you get capital the increase becomes more easy and rapid; but one who has capital is already rich, and does not need to consider how to become so. No matter how poor you may be, if you begin to do things in the Certain Way you will begin to get rich; and you will begin to have capital. The getting of capital is a part of the process of getting rich; and it is a part of the result which invariably follows the doing of things in the Certain Way. You may be the poorest man on the continent, and be deeply in debt; you may have neither friends, influence, nor resources; but if you begin to do things in this way, you must infallibly begin to get rich, for like causes must produce like effects. If you have no capital, you can get capital; if you are in the wrong business, you can get into the right business; if you are in the wrong location, you can go to the right location; and you can do so **by beginning in your present business and in your present location** to do things in the Certain Way which causes success.

7

HOW RICHES COME TO YOU

When I say that you do not have to drive sharp bargains, I do not mean that you do not have to drive any bargains at all, or that you are above the necessity for having any dealings with your fellow men. I mean that you will not need to deal with them unfairly; you do not have to get something for nothing, **but can give to every man more than you take from him.**

You cannot give every man more in cash market value than you take from him, but you can give him more in use value than the cash value of the thing you take from him. The paper, ink, and other material in this book may not be worth the money you pay for it; but if the ideas suggested by it bring you thousands of dollars, you have not been wronged by those who sold it to you; they have given you a great use value for a small cash value.

Let us suppose that I own a picture by one of the great artists, which, in any civilized community, is worth thousands of dollars. I take it to Baffin Ray, and by "salesmanship" induce an Eskimo to give a bundle of furs worth $500 for it. I have really wronged him, for he has no use for the picture; it has no use value to him; it will not add to his life.

But suppose I give him a gun worth $50 for his furs; then he has made a good bargain. He has use for the gun; it will get him many more furs and much food; it will add to his life in every way; it will make him rich.

When you rise from the competitive to the creative plane, you can scan your business transactions very strictly, and if you are selling any man anything which does not add more to his life than the thing he gave you in exchange, you can afford to stop it. You do not have to beat anybody in business. And if you are in a business which does beat people, get out of it at once.

Give every man more in use value than you take from him in cash value; then you are adding to the life of the world by every business transaction.

If you have people working for you, you must take from them more in cash value than you pay them in wages; but you can so organize your business that it will be filled with the principle of advancement, and so that each employee who wishes to do so may advance a little every day.

You can make your business do for your employees what this book is doing for you. You can so conduct your business that it will be a sort of ladder, by which every employee who will take the trouble may climb to riches himself; and given the opportunity, if he will not do so it is not your fault.

And finally, because you are to cause the creation of your riches from Formless Substance which permeates all your environment, it does not follow that they are to take shape from the atmosphere and come into being before your eyes.

If you want a sewing machine, for instance, I do not mean

to tell you that you are to impress the thought of a sewing machine on Thinking Substance until the machine is formed without hands, in the room where you sit, or elsewhere. But if you want a sewing machine, hold the mental image of it with the most positive certainty that it is being made, or is on its way to you. After once forming the thought, have the most absolute and unquestioning faith that the sewing machine is coming; never think of it, or speak, of it, in any other way than as being sure to arrive. Claim it as already yours.

It will be brought to you by the power of the Supreme Intelligence, acting upon the minds of men. If you live in Maine, it may be that a man will be brought from Texas or Japan to engage in some transaction which will result in your getting what you want.

If so, the whole matter will be as much to that man's advantage as it is to yours.

Do not forget for a moment that the Thinking Substance is through all, in all, communicating with all, and can influence all. The desire of Thinking Substance for fuller life and better living has caused the creation of all the sewing machines already made; and it can cause the creation of millions more, and will, whenever men set it in motion by desire and faith, and by acting in a Certain Way.

You can certainly have a sewing machine in your house; and it is just as certain that you can have any other thing or things which you want, and which you will use for the advancement of your own life and the lives of others.

You need not hesitate about asking largely; "it is your Father's pleasure to give you the kingdom," said Jesus.

Original Substance wants to live all that is possible in you, and wants you to have all that you can or will use for the living of the most abundant life.

If you fix upon your consciousness the fact that the desire you feel for the possession of riches is one with the desire of Omnipotence for more complete expression, your faith becomes invincible.

Once I saw a little boy sitting at a piano, and vainly trying to bring harmony out of the keys; and I saw that he was grieved and provoked by his inability to play real music. I asked him the cause of his vexation, and he answered, "I can feel the music in me, but I can't make my hands go right." The music in him was the URGE of Original Substance, containing all the possibilities of all life; all that there is of music was seeking expression through the child.

God, the One Substance, is trying to live and do and enjoy things through humanity. He is saying "I want hands to build wonderful structures, to play divine harmonies, to paint glorious pictures; I want feet to run my errands, eyes to see my beauties, tongues to tell mighty truths and to sing marvelous songs," and so on.

All that there is of possibility is seeking expression through men. God wants those who can play music to have pianos and every other instrument, and to have the means to cultivate their talents to the fullest extent; He wants those who can appreciate beauty to be able to surround themselves with beautiful things; He wants those who can discern truth to have every opportunity to travel and observe; He wants those who can appreciate dress to be beautifully clothed, and those who can appreciate good food to be luxuriously fed.

He wants all these things because it is Himself that enjoys

and appreciates them; it is God who wants to play, and sing, and enjoy beauty, and proclaim truth and wear fine clothes, and eat good foods. "It is God that worketh in you to will and to do," said Paul.

The desire you feel for riches is the infinite, seeking to express Himself in you as He sought to find expression in the little boy at the piano.

So you need not hesitate to ask largely.

Your part is to focalize and express the desire to God.

This is a difficult point with most people; they retain something of the old idea that poverty and self-sacrifice are pleasing to God. They look upon poverty as a part of the plan, a necessity of nature. They have the idea that God has finished His work, and made all that He can make, and that the majority of men must stay poor because there is not enough to go around. They hold to so much of this erroneous thought that they feel ashamed to ask for wealth; they try not to want more than a very modest competence, just enough to make them fairly comfortable.

I recall now the case of one student who was told that he must get in mind a clear picture of the things he desired, so that the creative thought of them might be impressed on Formless Substance. He was a very poor man, living in a rented house, and having only what he earned from day to day; and he could not grasp the fact that all wealth was his. So, after thinking the matter over, he decided that he might reasonably ask for a new rug for the floor of his best room, and an anthracite coal stove to heat the house during the cold weather. Following the instructions given in this book, he obtained these things in a few months; and then it dawned upon him that he had not asked enough. He went through the house in which he lived, and planned all the improvements he would like to make in it; he mentally added a bay window here and a room there, until it was complete in his mind as his ideal home; and then he planned its furnishings.

Holding the whole picture in his mind, he began living in the Certain Way, and moving toward what he wanted; and he owns the house now, and is rebuilding it after the form of his mental image. And now, with still larger faith, he is going on to get greater things. It has been unto him according to his faith, and it is so with you and with all of us.

8

GETTING INTO THE RIGHT BUSINESS

Success, in any particular business, depends for one thing upon your possessing in a well-developed state the faculties required in that business.

Without good musical faculty no one can succeed as a teacher of music; without well-developed mechanical faculties no one can achieve great success in any of the mechanical trades; without tact and the commercial faculties no one can succeed in mercantile pursuits. But to possess in a well-developed state the faculties required in your particular vocation does not insure getting rich. There are musicians who have remarkable talent, and who yet remain poor; there are blacksmiths, carpenters, and so on who have excellent mechanical ability, but who do not get rich; and there are merchants with good faculties for dealing with men who nevertheless fail.

The different faculties are tools; it is essential to have good tools, but it is also essential that the tools should be used in the Right Way. One man can take a sharp saw, a square, a good plane, and so on, and build a handsome article of furniture; another man can take the same tools and set to work to duplicate the article, but his production will be a botch. He does not know how to use good tools in a successful way.

The various faculties of your mind are the tools with which you must do the work which is to make you rich; it will be easier for you to succeed if you get into a business for which you are well equipped with mental tools.

Generally speaking, you will do best in that business which will use your strongest faculties; the one for which you are naturally "best fitted." But there are limitations to this statement, also. No man should regard his vocation as being irrevocably fixed by the tendencies with which he was born.

You can get rich in ANY business, for if you have not the right talent for you can develop that talent; it merely means that you will have to make your tools as you go along, instead of confining yourself to the use of those with which you were born. It will be EASIER for you to succeed in a vocation for which you already have the talents in a well-developed state; but you CAN succeed in any vocation, for you can develop any rudimentary talent, and there is no talent of which you have not at least the rudiment.

You will get rich most easily in point of effort, if you do that for which you are best fitted; but you will get rich most satisfactorily if you do that which you WANT to do.

Doing what you want to do is life; and there is no real satisfaction in living if we are compelled to be forever doing something which we do not like to do, and can never do what we want to do. And it is certain that you can do what you want to do; the desire to do it is proof that you have within you the power which can do it.

Desire is a manifestation of power.

The desire to play music is the power which can play music seeking expression and development; the desire to invent mechanical devices is the mechanical talent seeking expression and development.

Where there is no power, either developed or undeveloped, to do a thing, there is never any desire to do that thing; and where there is strong desire to do a thing, it is certain proof that the power to do it is strong, and only requires to be developed and applied in the Right Way.

All things else being equal, it is best to select the business for which you have the best developed talent; but if you have a strong desire to engage in any particular line of work, you should select that work as the ultimate end at which you aim.

You can do what you want to do, and it is your right and privilege to follow the business or vocation which will be most congenial and pleasant.

You are not obliged to do what you do not like to do, and should not do it except as a means to bring you to the doing of the thing you want to do.

If there are past mistakes whose consequences have placed you in an undesirable business or environment, you maybe obliged for some time to do what you do not like to do; but you can make the doing of it pleasant by knowing that it is making it possible for you to come to the doing of what you want to do.

If you feel that you are not in the right vocation, do not act too hastily in trying to get into another one. The best way, generally, to change business or environment is by growth.

Do not be afraid to make a sudden and radical change if the opportunity is presented, and you feel after careful consideration that it is the right opportunity; but never take sudden or radical action when you are in doubt as to the wisdom of doing so.

There is never any hurry on the creative plane; and there is no lack of opportunity.

When you get out of the competitive mind you will understand that you never need to act hastily. No one else is going to beat you to the thing you want to do; there is enough for all. If one space is taken, another and a better one will be opened for you a little farther on; there is plenty of time. When you are in doubt, wait. Fall back on the contemplation of your vision, and increase your faith and purpose; and by all means, in times of doubt and indecision, cultivate gratitude.

A day or two spent in contemplating the vision of what you want, and in earnest thanksgiving that you are getting it, will bring your mind into such close relationship with the Supreme that you will make no mistake when you do act.

There is a mind which knows all there is to know; and you can come into close unity with this mind by faith and the purpose to advance in life, if you have deep gratitude.

Mistakes come from acting hastily, or from acting in fear or doubt, or in forgetful ness of the Right Motive, which is more life to all, and less to none.

As you go on in the Certain Way, opportunities will come to you in increasing number; and you will need to be very steady in your faith and purpose, and to keep in close touch with the All Mind by reverent gratitude.

Do all that you can do in a perfect manner every day, but

do it without haste, worry, or fear. Go as fast as you can, but never hurry.

Remember that in the moment you begin to hurry you cease to be a creator and become a competitor; you drop back upon the old plane again.

Whenever you find yourself hurrying, call a halt; fix your attention on the mental image of the thing you want, and begin to give thanks that you are getting it. The exercise of GRATITUDE will never fail to strengthen your faith and renew your purpose.

9

THE ADVANCING MAN

What I have said in the last chapter applies as well to the professional man and the wage-earner as to the man who is engaged in mercantile business.

No matter whether you are a physician, a teacher, or a clergyman, if you can give increase of life to others and make them sensible of the fact, they will be attracted to you, and you will get rich. The physician who holds the vision of himself as a great and successful healer, and who works toward the complete realization of that vision with faith and purpose, as described in former chapters, will come into such close touch with the Source of Life that he will be phenomenally successful; patients will come to him in throngs.

No one has a greater opportunity to carry into effect the teaching of this book than the practitioner of medicine; it does not matter to which of the various schools he may belong, for the principle of healing is common to all of them, and maybe reached by all alike. The Advancing Man in medicine, who holds to a clear mental image of himself as successful, and who obeys the laws of faith, purpose, and gratitude, will cure every curable case he undertakes, no matter what remedies he may use.

In the field of religion, the world cries out for the clergyman who can teach his hearers the true science of abundant life. He who masters the details of the science of getting rich, together with the allied sciences of being well, of being great, and of winning love, and who teaches these details from the pulpit, will never lack for a congregation. This is the gospel that the world needs; it will give increase of life, and men will hear it gladly, and will give liberal support to the man who brings it to them.

What is now needed is a demonstration of the science of life from the pulpit. We want preachers who can not only tell us how, but who in their own persons will show us how. We need the preacher who will himself be rich, healthy, great, and beloved, to teach us how to attain to these things; and when he comes he will find a numerous and loyal following.

The same is true of the teacher who can inspire the children with the faith and purpose of the advancing life. He will never be "out of a job." And any teacher who has this faith and purpose can give it to his pupils; he cannot help giving it to them if it is part of his own life and practice.

What is true of the teacher, preacher, and physician is true of the lawyer, dentist, real estate man, insurance agent—of everybody.

The combined mental and personal action I have described is infallible; it cannot fail. Every man and woman who follows these instructions steadily, perseveringly, and to the letter, will get rich. The law of the Increase of Life is as mathematically certain in its operation as the law of gravitation; getting rich is an exact science.

The wage-earner will find this as true of his case as of any of the others mentioned. Do not feel that you have no chance to get rich because you are working where there is no visible opportunity for advancement, where wages are small and the cost of living high. Form your clear mental vision of what you want, and begin to act with faith and purpose.

Do all the work you can do, every day, and do each piece of work in a perfectly successful manner; put the power of success, and the purpose to get rich, into everything that you do.

But do not do this merely with the idea of currying favor with your employer, in the hope that he, or those above you, will see your good work and advance you; it is not likely that they will do so.

The man who is merely a "good" workman, filling his place to the very best of his ability, and satisfied with that, is valuable to his employer; and it is not to the employer's interest to promote him; he is worth more where he is.

To secure advancement, something more is necessary than to be too large for your place.

The man who is certain to advance is the one who is too big for his place, and who has a clear concept of what he wants to be; who knows that he can become what he wants to be and who is determined to BE what he wants to be.

Do not try to more than fill your present place with a view to pleasing your employer; do it with the idea of advancing yourself. Hold the faith and purpose of increase during work hours, after work hours, and before work hours. Hold it in such a way that every person who comes in contact with you, whether foreman, fellow workman, or social acquaintance, will feel the power of purpose radiating from you; so that every one will get the sense of advancement and increase from you. Men will be attracted to you, and if there is no possibility for advancement in your present job, you will very soon see an opportunity to take another job.

There is a Power which never fails to present opportunity to the Advancing Man who is moving in obedience to law.

God cannot help helping you, if you act in a Certain Way; He must do so in order to help Himself.

There is nothing in your circumstances or in the industrial situation that can keep you down. If you cannot get rich working for the steel trust, you can get rich on a ten-acre farm; and if you begin to move in the Certain Way, you will certainly escape from the "clutches" of the steel trust and get on to the farm or wherever else you wish to be.

If a few thousands of its employees would enter upon the Certain Way, the steel trust would soon be in a bad plight; it would have to give its workingmen more opportunity, or go out of business. Nobody has to work for a trust; the trusts can keep men in so called hopeless conditions only so long as there are men who are too ignorant to know of the science of getting rich, or too intellectually slothful to practice it.

Begin this way of thinking and acting, and your faith and purpose will make you quick to see any opportunity to better your condition.

Such opportunities will speedily come, for the Supreme, working in All, and working for you, will bring them before you.

Do not wait for an opportunity to be all that you want to be; when an opportunity to be more than you are now is presented and you feel impelled toward it, take it. It will be the first step toward a greater opportunity.

There is no such thing possible in this universe as a lack of opportunities for the man who is living the advancing life.

It is inherent in the constitution of the cosmos that all things shall be for him and work together for his good; and he must certainly get rich if he acts and thinks in the Certain Way. So let wage-earning men and women study this book with great care, and enter with confidence upon the course of action it prescribes; it will not fail.